PENGUIN BOOKS

QUIRKY QWERTY

Torbjörn Lundmark was born in Sweden and now lives in Australia. He studied linguistics and Slavonic languages at the University of Uppsala and spent one year at the philological faculty at Voronezh University in the former Soviet Union. He is a professional writer, illustrator, and cartoonist, and is the author of several books, including children's books. He is a lover of languages and is currently learning to read and write Chinese.

Quirky QWERTY

A Note
on the
Type

Torbjörn Lundmark

PENGUIN BOOKS

FOR D.K.

THE KEY TO MY HAPPINESS

PENGUIN BOOKS
Published by the Penguin Group
Penguin Group (USA) Inc., 375 Hudson Street,
New York, New York 10014, U.S.A.
Penguin Books Ltd, 80 Strand, London WC2R 0RL, England
Penguin Books Australia Ltd, 250 Camberwell Road, Camberwell,
Victoria 3124, Australia
Penguin Books Canada Ltd, 10 Alcorn Avenue, Toronto, Ontario,
Canada M4V 3B2
Penguin Books India (P) Ltd, 11 Community Centre, Panchsheel Park,
New Delhi – 110 017, India
Penguin Books (N.Z.) Ltd, Cnr Rosedale and Airborne Roads,
Albany, Auckland, New Zealand
Penguin Books (South Africa) (Pty) Ltd, 24 Sturdee Avenue, Rosebank,
Johannesburg 2196, South Africa

Penguin Books Ltd, Registered Offices:
80 Strand, London WC2R 0RL, England

First published in Australia by University of New South Wales Press Ltd 2002
First published in the United States of America in Penguin Books 2003

10 9 8 7 6 5 4 3 2 1

Copyright © Torbjörn Lundmark, 2002
All rights reserved

ISBN 0 86840 436 5 (hc.)
ISBN 0 14 20.0270 4 (pbk.)
CIP data available

Printed in the United States of America
Designed by Di Quick

Acknowledgments

Thanks to Sheil Land Associates for their permission to use Eric Partridge's Comic Alphabets, and to the Master and Fellows of Pembroke College, Cambridge, for manuscript transcripts. Picture credits are due to the United States Trademarks and Patents Office, to Darryl Rehr and his typewriter cyber-site, to the European Commission, and to the Tekniska Museet in Stockholm.

I also wish to thank D.K. for all her wonderful inspiration, and Di Quick for the original seed and the subsequent outstanding design.

I am indebted to many others for their assistance in my research: Lennart Bäckman, Kjell Carli, Phil Davies, Leif Ekman, Våge Landberg, Garth Tomkinson and Zhang Jun Xia among them.

I owe my gratitude to the editor Roderick Campbell, for his knowledge and advice. Without his great contribution, the reversed comma might never have made it into print again.

A	B	C	D	E	F	G	H	I	J	K	L	M
71	98	94	77	59	80	94	84	65	65	86	88	102

!	@	#	$	%	&	*	()	[]	{}	_	-	+-
106	108	111	113	116	117	119	121	121	121	123	125	127

Cont

	O	P	Q	R	S	T	U	V	W	X	Y	Z
00	68	69	57	61	74	63	80	80	80	92	65	90

	|	:	;	' '	,	.	?	/		§¶	†	€
28	129	132	134	135	141	144	146	149	152	155	157	159

ents

Introd

The QWERTY keyboard hasn't been around for long, yet it has revolutionised the way we work and the way we live. Its arrangement has become as familiar as the clock-face and the telephone dial. It has brought about a fundamental change in the way we communicate — in business and commerce, in government and politics, in the press and electronic media, in printing and publishing, in schools and universities, even in personal correspondence.

The keyboard is a quirky thing. It has become the main tool of the cyber-age, yet it has barely changed since the 1870s; it is a marvel of design economy, yet it contains many characters that most people never use; it doesn't even present the alphabet in alphabetical order, yet many nine-year-olds know it better than their

ABC.

...ction

Listen to the tapping of keys: at this very moment, billions of keys on millions of keyboards around the globe are being used to type messages — however loving or hateful, dull or engrossing, trivial or monumentally life-changing.

This is the story of those keys and the characters they produce. This is not a scientific work. In fact, nothing in this book can be said to be absolutely true. Even if it *were* a scientific book this fact would not change. Scholars still argue about the origins of the alphabet and what the letters signify, and why the numbers look the way they do, and how all the other characters that appear in these pages came about. What is undeniably true is that the keys on the keyboard reach far into the past and, depending on which order you press them, have the power to change the future.

Mill tc

BORROW AND PINCH, TINKER AND TWEAK

'The pen is mightier than the sword', Edward Bulwer-Lytton wrote. Perhaps it is not so strange, then, that every wordsmith has a gunsmith to thank for the first typewriter.

Many a war of words has been fought with a Remington, and it was indeed the E. Remington & Sons Arms Company in Ilion, New York State, United States of America, that manufactured the first commercially available typewriter. The year was 1874.

The gun-maker's newest weapon had a name that somehow missed the mark. It was called 'The Sholes & Glidden Type Writer'. The marketing of this finicky, clunky contraption was equally off-target: only 5000 were ever sold. They retailed for US$125 and were sold from the world's first typewriter shop, at 4 Hanover Street in New York.

But if the name was lame, the calibre wasn't. The apparatus was like the Big Bertha cannon in stature and bulk: it was big, it was heavy. It was an unwieldy, cumbrous behemoth with a monstrous metal hulk mounted on a table with wrought-iron legs and a treadle at the bottom. It looked like a sewing-machine.

Sholes

The contraption rolled into a writer's study with the same difficulty as its name rolled off the tongue.

While the hands did the typing, the feet operated the carriage return. Typing with the Sholes & Glidden Type Writer Model I was like playing a church organ: it went to all extremities.

Why was it designed this way? Because Remington had come upon bad times; the American Civil War was over, and the Wild West wasn't all that wild anymore. The demand for guns and rifles was waning, and Remington had to look for greener pastures. A new manufacturing branch was set up, producing farm equipment and sewing-machines. Remington signed a contract with Sholes to manufacture the typewriter he had patented. Two

The Sholes & Glidden
Type Writer Model I

of Remington's sewing-machine mechanics, William Jenne and Jefferson Clough, were then put to the task of making Sholes's contrivance suitable for the production line. Jenne and Clough had one strength in common: a solid knowledge of sewing-machines, and so the first 1000 'Type Writers' used the base, stand and foot-pedal of a Remington sewing-machine.

INVENTORS

The Sholes and Glidden Type Writer was invented by three men: Christopher Latham Sholes, Carlos Glidden and Samuel W. Soulé. Soulé's name was quickly forgotten and didn't even appear on the proud brand-plaque of the machine. Glidden's name did appear, but few people today connect his name with typewriters. It is Christopher Latham Sholes who usually — and erroneously — is hailed as the inventor of the typewriter.

The idea had occurred to Sholes in 1864, when he and Soulé had been issued a patent for a page-numbering machine. It was Carlos Glidden who sowed the first seed in Sholes's mind: if a machine could place page numbers on the paper, why not the letters of the alphabet as well? Sholes became so besotted with the idea that it became his life mission: he kept tinkering with his machine until his death in 1890.

Yet Sholes cannot be said to be the inventor of the first type-writing machine. That honour goes to the Englishman Henry Mill, a prominent 'engineer to the New River Water Company', who also liked to spend his time tinkering with new ideas, and had been granted a British patent for a kind of type-writing machine already in 1714. The patent, No. 395, was issued on 7 January of that year. According to the documents, Mr Mill had:

… *by his great study, paines and expense, lately invented and brought to perfection an artificial machine or method for the impressing or transcribing of letters singly or progressively one after another, as in writing, whereby all writing whatever may be engrossed in paper or parchment so neat & exact as not to be distinguished from print.*

Another patent was lodged by an American, William Austin Burt. In 1829 he designed a machine that had type arranged on a semi-circular wheel which was turned to the relevant letter and then pressed against the paper.

The first inventor to use individual type-bars for each letter was a Frenchman, Xavier Progin, in 1833.

At least fifty-two typewriters are known to have been designed prior to Sholes's model. Several machines were built with piano keyboards, and had names like *cembalo scrivano* ('writing harpsichord') and *clavier imprimeur* ('piano printer'). The variety of mechanisms was as wide-ranging as the backgrounds of their inventors: typewriters were designed by blacksmiths and professors of physics, German barons and Austrian counts, teachers and printers, lawyers and physicians, watchmakers and electricians.

Interestingly, most of the early designs had nothing to do with a desire to mechanise handwriting: instead, their purpose was to make reading possible for blind people. The idea was to provide deeply embossed letters that could be read by running sensitive fingertips over the text. Only later came the notion that typing could replace handwriting.

Sholes himself relied heavily on previous designs, such as one by John Pratt of London and an 1843 invention by an American, Charles Grover Thurber, of an escapement mechanism that was suitable for forwarding the carriage one notch after each letter was imprinted.

SINGLE-BUTTON OPERATION

Christopher Latham Sholes's first brainchild was a strange contraption with only one key and one letter (W). The type-bar was suspended from a metal ring above the single key. For his demonstration model Sholes used a Morse telegraph key.

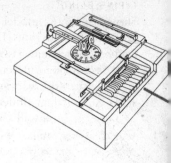

Typing was done by lining up the letter with the Morse key, and then striking it. This resulted in the type-bar swinging upwards to hit an arrangement composed of a piece of carbon paper with a sheet of writing paper, backed by a piece of glass.

Drawing from Sholes's 1868 patent, using a piano-key arrangement

This could hardly be called touch-typing and provided little indication of the technical revolution that was to follow. But it was enough to show that Sholes's idea did work. He went on to add the rest of the letters, and started using piano keys for a keyboard of sorts.

The contraption was enough to spark the interest of one James Densmore, who provided some financial backing for further development of Sholes's wonderful machine. Reportedly, Densmore was a shabbily dressed, unkempt man, nevertheless full of unbridled enthusiasm for the project. Sholes himself was a shy and withdrawn person, and had it not been for Densmore's effusive spruiking of the typewriter to Philo Remington, the whole project might have come to nothing: Sholes was not the type.

Densmore contributed US$600 in return for a share in the invention. Not until later did Sholes learn that the investment had cost Densmore every last penny of his life savings.

Sholes's patented model was a quantum leap from his fumbling first attempts. The machine had almost all the features and characteristics of a modern typewriter — with one major difference. In the patented machine, the type-bars swung upwards and struck the paper underneath the platen. This meant that all the action took place deep inside the belly of the beast: the operator could not see what was being typed.

This minor detail was at first solved by using a hinged carriage, so that the typist could swing the entire assembly upwards (like the cabin of a Mack truck) and peek inside to see the written words.

Obviously, this was a rather irksome inconvenience to the operator; so much so that the machine came to be commonly known as a 'blind-writer'.

Typists were left to type in the dark for some ten years before the machine was redesigned and the bank of type bars turned around in order to strike the paper from the front, thus letting operators see the result of their work as they typed.

It has been claimed (even by the man himself) that Mark Twain wrote Tom Sawyer on a Remington. This is probably not true. What is true is that Twain was the first author to present a typewritten manuscript to his publisher. This was for the novel *Life on the Mississippi* in 1883. But he didn't type it himself: he used a typist to transcribe his handwritten manuscript.

Nevertheless, the wheels were turning, the cranks cranking, and the typewriter was a fact: the way we saw writing had begun to shift.

In 1874 Mark Twain tried out his newly acquired 'Type Writer' for the first time. He typed a letter to his brother:

BJUIT KIOR M LKJHGFDSA:QWERTYUIOP:_-CBV64320 BT
                                                        HA
                                    HARTFORD, DEC. 9,
DEAR BROTHER:
I AM TRYING T TO GET THE HANG OF THIS NEW F
FANGLED WRITING MACHINE, BUT AM NOT MAKING
A SHINING SUCCESS OF IT. HOWEVER THIS IS THE
FIRST ATTEMPT I EVER HAVE MADE, & YET I PER-
CEIVETHAT I SHALL SOON & EASILY ACQUIRE A FINE
FACILITY IN ITS USE. I SAW THE THING IN BOS-
TON THE OTHER DAY & WAS GREATLY TAKEN WITH
IT. SUSIE HAS STRUCK THE KEYS ONCE OR TWICE,
& NO DOUBT HAS PRINTED SOME LETTERS WHICH DO
NOT BELONG WHERE SHE PUT THEM.
THE HAVING BEEN A COMPOSITOR IS LIKELY TO BE
A GREAT HELP TO ME,SINCE O NE CHIEFLY NEEDS
SWIFTNESS IN BANGING THE KEYS.THE MACHINE COSTS
125 DOLLARS.THE MACHINE HAS SEVERAL VIRTUES
I BELIEVE IT WILL PRINT FASTER THAN I CAN WRITE.
ONE MAY LEAN BACK IN HIS CHAIR & WORK IT. IT
PILES AN AWFUL STACK OF WORDS ON ONE PAGE.
IT DON'T MUSS THINGS OR SCATTER INK BLOTS AROUND.
OF COURSE IT SAVES PAPER.

                                    SUSIE IS GONE,
NOW, & I FANCY I SHALL MAKE BETTER PROGRESS.
WORKING THIS TYPE-WRITER REMINDS ME OF OLD
ROBERT BUCHANAN, WHO, YOU REMEMBER, USED TO
SET UP ARTICLES AT THE CASE WITHOUT PREVIOUS-
LY PUTTING THEM IN THE FORM OF MANUSCRIPT.I
WAS LOST IN ADMIRATION OF SUCH MARVELOUS
INTELLECTUAL CAPACITY.

                            LOVE TO MOLLIE.
                        YOUR BROTHER,
                            SAM.

WHY QWERTY?

Christopher Latham Sholes might not have been the inventor of the typewriter, but he was certainly the first person ever to spell QWERTY.

Why did he place the keys in such a quirky arrangement?

Sholes's first tentative design for a writing-machine had an alphabetic keyboard layout: the keys ran from A to Z in two rows.

But he had a problem.

His prototype-writer was a rather crudely made device, manufactured by the toolmakers employed at the Kleinstuber machine shop in Milwaukee. Milwaukee was a small, backwoods timber town in the 1860s. The toolmakers he dealt with were perhaps highly skilled, but didn't have the right tools: they were more accustomed to axe-grinding than type-wrighting.

The problem was that his typewriter components were so coarsely crafted that when two adjacent type-bars were used in quick succession, they tended to stick and jam the mechanism.

Sholes discovered that many English words contained combinations of letters next to each other in the alphabet. This included very common words such as bUT, ABle, HIGH, and countless other word STRings.

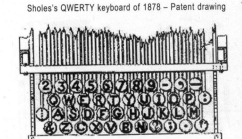

Sholes's QWERTY keyboard of 1878 – Patent drawing

His solution was as simple as it was ingenious: move common letter-pairs away from each other.

He went about the task in a scientific way. He got the educator Amos Densmore (his sponsor's brother) to prepare a frequency study of letter-pairs in the English language. He then used the study to split up as many common letter-combinations as he could and scatter them across his keyboard.

When he was finished, the result was the alphabet soup that is the QWERTY keyboard. It was a messy keyboard, but at least the mess wasn't sticky.

ALTERNATIVE KEYBOARDS
(letter keys only)

Dvořak keyboard 1932

P	Y	F	G	C	R	L

| A | O | E | U | I | D | H | T | N | S |

| Q | J | K | X | B | M | W | V | Z |

Caligraph keyboard 1880

| V | W | | | | | | J | K |

| R | T | E | | q | z | | U | G | H |

| A | S | w | t | r | e | y | u | i | o | I | O |

| D | F | a | s | d | f | g | h | c | k | N | L |

| B | C | j | x | v | b | n | l | m | p | M | P |

| Q | X | | | | | | Y | Z |

Prouty keyboard 1888

V	X	Z	Q

| W | Y | K | B | N | P | L | F | J |

| G | I | S | U | C |

| O | T | H | M | A | R | E | D |

Ideal (DHIATENSOR) keyboard 1893

Z	X	K	G	B	V	Q	J

| P | W | F | U | L | C | M | Y |

| D | H | I | A | T | E | N | S | O | R |

Fitch keyboard 1886

X	B	M	R	N	G	T	L	P

| J | W | O | A | E | I | U | K | Q |

| V | S | D | H | O | Y | F | C | Z |

In our modern times of computers and electronics rather than mechanics, why haven't keyboards reverted to alphabetical order? There is no reason to worry about sticky type-bars anymore. So, why are we still stuck with the QWERTY keyboard?

Economists, politicians and planners have a name for it: 'the Qwerty effect'. It means that it often seems better to stick to old standards than to invent new ways, even if the new ways are more efficient.

The Qwerty effect has prevailed over several attempts at making typing freer, friendlier and faster to master.

Among these, there was the Dvořak keyboard that had all the vowels and the six most common consonants on the same centre row. There was also the 'DHIATENSOR', the 'Scientific', the 'MALTRON' and the 'Palantype', along with many others.

Perhaps QWERTY's rivals were ergonomically sound; maybe they made a slight difference in typing speed. But the Qwerty effect applies: why suddenly learn a *new* keyboard layout? Besides, a far simpler fact holds true: good typists type fast, and poor typists do not.

And, so, to this day Sholes's quirky QWERTY remains the norm.

Whether by intent or accident, the keyboard layout had one additional advantage: Remington sales representatives with no knowledge of this strange, newfangled hive of rods and levers and cogs and springs could easily demonstrate what it did, how it worked — even what it was called — by using their index finger to pick out in letters only from the top row:

T Y P E W R I T E R

A to Z

AS EASY AS BC

How old is the alphabet? As a set of twenty-six letters, the alphabet we use to write English is not very old at all. None of the letters were fully differentiated until the 1800s, less than two hundred years ago.

But the history of the letters of the alphabet and why they look the way they do is a long string of developments, dating back many thousands of years.

What is an alphabet? In short, it is a set of signs, each of which stands for one basic sound in a language. String them together in the correct order, and you get words.

BRUSH UP YOUR EGYPTIAN

The Egyptians did not use an alphabet as their writing system. Yet, they wrote extensively, and left behind a lot of written material about their life. They had their own unique writing system: the hieroglyphs.

Most hieroglyphs are pictures of things in the world. Amongst the rows and columns of hieroglyphic writing you will recognise a wide variety of birds and animals, insects and fishes, flowers and plants, utensils and tools, people and parts of the body, sky and earth and water, buildings and furniture, and many others.

The hieroglyphs had various functions: sometimes they meant exactly what they depicted; usually they signified phonetic sounds based on the word for the thing they depicted; and often they served as flags, indicating a category or context that had to do with what they depicted.

CHINESE WHISKERS

The brush-strokes of Chinese calligraphy also make up pictures, albeit in a much more stylised manner compared with hieroglyphs. You can't really 'guess' what an unfamiliar Chinese character stands for just by looking at it. Still, certain Chinese characters do look a little like their meanings. With a bit of imagination, the sign for 'rain', for example, looks like water-drops falling down from a heavy sky 雨 . The same goes for 'tree' 木 (canopy, trunk and roots), 'river' 川 (flowing water), 'mountain' 山 (peaks), 'mouth' 口 (a hole), and many other basic words.

Then the abstractions go a little deeper: 'big' 大 is

a person with legs apart and arms outstretched, as if showing the size of the fish that got away.

Even more abstract, the character for 'trust' 信 is a combination of 'person' beside the sign for 'word' (to stand by your word). The sign for 'rest' 休 is a person next to a tree (to lean against a tree trunk). The sun 日 and the moon 月 together make the word for 'bright' 明 . 'Left' and 'right' are also good examples. 'Left' 左 is a hand holding a ruler or set-square (most people hold the ruler down with their left hand and draw the line with the other). 'Right' 右 is a hand and a mouth (most chopstick-users put food into the mouth using the right hand).

Because each individual character in a non-alphabetic writing system has a separate meaning or function, a lot of characters must be learnt. To read a newspaper in Chinese, you must know around 2000 characters; to read a modern novel, perhaps twice that. Chinese word-processing software has around 13,000 characters. Anyone who has seen a Chinese typewriter would understand how unwieldy such a writing system is.

This was also the case in ancient Egypt: writing was complex, time-consuming and difficult to learn. It was hard to remember all the characters. Classical Egyptian had about 700 hieroglyphs. This number grew considerably over time. No wonder scribes who knew their mettle were regarded as people of high rank in Egyptian society.

A FOR ACROPHONY

About 3500 years ago, on the eastern shores of the Mediterranean, somebody with a sharp mind and a short memory, perhaps a Phoenician, had an idea: let's forget about learning hundreds upon hundreds of stylised pictures with their own individual functions. Why not start writing our entire language with a new system of 'letters', each standing for one single sound?

How do we do that? Easy: we'll do it acrophonical-ly! the Phoenician said (but perhaps not in those terms). Out of all the hieroglyphs, we pick a few and forget about their pictorial meaning, but treat them as the first sound of the object they depict in our language. Say, *B* for 'building', *C* for 'camel', *D* for 'door', and so on.

This was a monumental mental leap in the very idea of writing. A character that looked like a door and was pronounced like 'door' no longer had anything to do with either the object or the name for it. Instead, it only signified the 'd' sound, and could be used in any word with that sound.

The new system was a success. As the centuries went by, the selected alphabetic characters that used to be hieroglyphs started to change: they became more and more stylised and began to look less and less like the 'pictures' they once were. After all, they didn't need to *look* like anything: now they only represented sounds, not things.

N VWLS

However, this new way of thinking and writing was not as easy as ABC, simply because the North Semitic alphabet, as it is known, did not have A or any other vowels.

Even today, Semitic writing such as Arabic and Hebrew does not use vowels. In certain instances vow-els may be indicated by adding tiny marks above and below the written text (like accents in French), but normally they are not used at all.

Can a language have no vowels? Is that why Arabic sounds so guttural to non-Arab ears?

The answer to both these questions is no. There are and always were vowels in spoken Arabic, Hebrew and Phoenician. But vowels play a much less important role in Semitic languages than they do in, say, English.

Whereas in English the words *mate, mite, mete, mote* and *mute* mean totally different things, Semitic languages depend on strings of consonants, not vowels. For example the string *k-t-b*, which has to do with writing:

HOW IT IS PRONOUNCED	WHAT IT MEANS	HOW IT IS WRITTEN
katab	he wrote	*ktb*
katabi	I wrote	*ktb*
katebu	they wrote	*ktb*
ketob	write	*ktb*
koteb	writing	*ktb*
katub	being written	*ktb*

And so it was with North Semitic: its alphabet contained only consonants; although vowels were well within earshot, not one of them was within sight.

IT'S NOT AT ALL GREEK TO ME!

The North Semitic alphabet was used around the eastern Mediterranean for a thousand years or so, before the Greeks saw it and decided to make use of it.

There was a problem, though: Phoenician was a Semitic language; Greek was an Indo-European one. In Greek, vowels were very important. Vowel-lessness might have been all right for the Phoenicians, but writing Greek without the vowels was like cooking moussaka without the lamb.

Another problem was that the North Semitic alphabet contained a lot of letters for sounds that were completely foreign to the Greek.

In short, to the Greeks, the North Semitic alphabet was both insufficient and superfluous at the same time.

THE GREAT GREEK TWEAK

Now something interesting happened. Instead of designing new characters for the sounds and vowels they needed, the Greeks simply assigned new sounds to some of the North Semitic letters that to them were useless.

This reassignment has often been described as a stroke of genius. However, perhaps it was simply the natural thing to do: a case of taking the script of one language and making it work for a completely different one — in other words, trimming square pegs until they fit into round holes.

ALPHA, BETA

Thanks to the Greeks, the alphabet now had both vowels and consonants, and could be used for writing non-Semitic languages.

It is interesting to note that the vowels you use on your keyboard are around a thousand years younger than the consonants. And that all the vowels used to be consonants.

WRITING LEFT, RIGHT AND CENTRE

Why are all European languages written from left to right, while Arabic runs from right to left?

The Egyptians wrote in every which way:

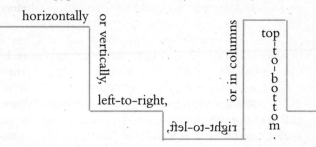

horizontally or vertically, left-to-right, right-to-left, or in columns top to bottom.

The only rule was to stick to the same direction throughout the text.

The North Semitic script favoured the horizontal right-to-left direction.

The Greeks couldn't decide. They wrote either left-to-right or right-to-left, often alternating the direction every other line. At the end of each line you went down one line and started writing in the opposite direction.

This type of back-and-forth writing is called 'boustrophedon', which literally means that you write as an ox ploughs a field: up one furrow, and down the next.

Often, the Greeks not only changed writing direction at the end of a line: on the way back, they mirror-reversed the letters themselves.

WE WRITE LIKE WOOF AND WEFT,

WE WRITE FROM LEFT TO RIGHT;

AND THEN WHAT'S LEFT TO WRITE,

WE WRITE FROM RIGHT TO LEFT!

WHEN IN ROME, DO AS THE ETRUSCANS DO

Around 700 BC, the Romans (who spoke Latin) borrowed the Greek alphabet and shaped it into their own. They probably did this in a roundabout way — by acquiring the alphabet from the Etruscans, who lived in what is now Tuscany and who used the Greek alphabet almost intact.

The greatness and magnificence commonly associated with Latin took its time to develop. For 600 years the new Latin alphabet was not used much at all. It was only around 100 BC that Latin writing began to show any signs of the grandeur to come.

The Romans adopted twenty-one letters, which they considered sufficient to write Latin. Their alphabet was the same as the modern English alphabet, excluding *J, U, W, Y* and *Z*.

ABC FOR KIDS

Perhaps the development of our alphabet from word-pictures to sound-symbols can be seen as a natural progression in humans.

Studies of children's learning to write have suggested that children go through many of the developmental stages our alphabet itself underwent.

In the earliest stages infants first find the connection between, say, a drawing of a cat and a particular real cat, such as Moggy, the family puss. The child sees a drawn image of a cat, points at the image, and says 'Moggy!'.

The next stage is to associate the drawing with the idea of the animal we know as a cat. The picture no longer represents Moggy the family pet, but any feline. The child points at the image and says, 'cat!'. The drawing has taken on the role of a hieroglyph.

When pictures of objects make way for written words, the child's understanding of how writing works develops in a similar way.

In the early acquisition of reading skills, the child often believes that a word must display in a *visual* way the characteristics of what the word means. For instance, 'snake' must be written with a long word because a snake is a long animal, and 'stars' is written with a lot of tiny words.

It is not until later in their development that children eventually grasp that writing represents words, not things.

Interestingly, once they have begun to understand that written words are made up of strings of letters, children often omit vowels in their writing: 'ball' might be written 'bl', 'cat' might be written 'kt', and so on. The realisation that words must use both consonants and vowels comes later.

WRITING HIGH AND LOW

Why are there two sets of characters in the Latin alphabet: upper-case and lower-case? And why are letter pairs such as *G—g* and *D—d* and *Q—q* so different?

Ancient Roman scripts had only capital letters, known as quadrata or square capitals. There were several writing styles, depending on the material you were writing on and the implements you used. The writing we know best is the lapidary style, a very straight-angled style which made it somewhat easier for the mason to chisel words into stone.

FORVM

Other styles included the elegant book capitals, which were still formal but slightly more rounded, and the rustic capitals, which were perhaps not as pleasing to the eye but quicker and easier to write. These were still formal scripts, but used in writing with a broad brush or pen. In short, the rustic style was the hand-written version of the chiselled lapidary style.

A cursive (running) style with rounder shapes and more flowing strings of letters developed for everyday writing with a pen on papyrus, and later on vellum or parchment. The Roman cursive style, although it still used only capitals, was to form the basis of our lower-case letters. One of the features of the Roman cursive style was the simplification of the square capitals by dropping parts of them, as in *b* losing the upper curve of *B*, and *h* discarding the upper right 'arm' of *H*.

A 4-stroke square capital rendered as a 2-stroke cursive capital

E ⇒ Є

Between the monumental lapidary script and the informal cursive script were several other styles that combined the characteristics of the two.

The use of pen and parchment led, in the 1st century AD, to a style using large, very rounded capitals, called uncial script (the name is relatively new, dating from the 18th century, and means 'inch-sized'). All uncial text was written in capitals only; there was no lower-case. It was based on the cursive capitals. The text was kept strictly between two guidelines. It was written with a broad pen, often held at an angle.

Between the 4th and 8th centuries, the uncials started to inch their way outside the rigid top-and-bottom guidelines of the capitals. This came to be known as semi-uncial or half-uncial script.

The half-uncial, or semi-uncial, script still comprised only capital letters, although they started to look a lot like our modern lower-case. Large letters in the older rustic style were often used as initials, with the following text bring written in half-uncials. The most beautiful half-uncial script, known as the Insular or Hiberno-Saxon script, started to develop in Ireland around AD 500 and made its way through the British Isles. It was used in such famous works as the *Book of Kells* and the *Lindisfarne Gospels.*

... AND ALONG COMES CHARLEMAGNE

The practice of using upper- and lower-case letters can be attributed to the Holy Roman emperor, Charlemagne (also known as Charles I, Carolus Magnus, Charles the Great, Karl der Grosse, among other names).

In the late 700s Charlemagne's vision was diffusion of knowledge. He set in motion an extensive educational program, in which ancient texts were to be copied into an easily readable format, and the Vulgate Bible and many liturgical texts were to be transcribed into authorised versions. The work was to be copied and made available to many other libraries, so that they could spread the word. This would mean rapid dissemination of knowledge across the empire.

To manage this massive task, the emperor appointed a scholar called Alcuin of York. Alcuin was persuaded to leave his beloved library at the cathedral school of York, first for the palace school of Aachen and then for the scriptorium at the Abbey of St Martin's at Tours.

Alcuin's work was to have a profound effect on Western writing. It is here that we first see the use of minuscules (lower-case letters) together with majuscules (upper-case). The clear, disciplined letters were as comfortable for the scribe to write as they were for the student to read.

The new lower-case letters came to be known as Carolingian or Caroline minuscules, named after Charlemagne (Carolus) himself. They became the foundation for our modern typefaces, many of which have scarcely changed from the original Carolingian letter-forms.

Only during one relatively short period since Alcuin's time has European type-style changed drastically (and then returned to its previous form). By the 14th century, a new style had developed, called black letter or fraktur script; it was also known as Old English and as Gothic script (perhaps this is why the script is nowadays often associated with horror films and tales of darkness). This distinctly angular script was created by holding a broad-nibbed pen at an angle and writing the character in a more compressed fashion. Black-letter script was used in northwestern Europe, including England, until the 16th century, and was used by Gutenberg in his **Frankenstein** printing press. Perhaps that is why fraktur was regularly used in Germany until the 1940s, and is sometimes still seen in certain German texts.

Most lower-case letters are simply smaller versions of their capital counterparts, such as *Cc, Oo, Pp, Ss, Vv*, and so on. Others have dropped a part of the capital, such as *Bb, Ll* and *Hh*. Yet some of the characters of the lower-case differ distinctly from the upper-case, for instance *Aa, Dd, Gg, Qq,* and *Rr.* This is because the capitals stem from the Roman monumental script, while the smaller letters are derived from the Roman cursive letters. These differences are explained in more detail later in this book, where their respective letters are dealt with.

JUST IN CASE

'Upper-case' and 'lower-case' are printer's terms. The typographer's job was to fit individual pieces of type, cast in metal, into a wooden frame to make up the text of a newspaper column or a page of a book. Each letter was picked up by hand and placed into the frame.

The metal type was kept on two trays, or cases, one above the other. The lower case held the minuscule type, which was used more frequently, and the upper case contained the capital letters, which were used less often.

KEYS TO PAST MYSTERIES

It is a common complaint that a computer grows old and obsolete even as you take it out the door of the shop where you bought it.

That might be so when it comes to circuit boards and microchips and hard disks. But not the keyboard: in a sense, you are still using 6000-year-old hieroglyphs as you type. Most, if not all of the alphabetic keys on a computer keyboard can be traced right back to what the pharaohs used to write.

But what about the other keys? The punctuation marks? The hashes and dashes and curls and twirls that are so handy for writing $%#★^!! expletives ... or for reaching someone@someplace.com?

Every button at your fingertip has a story to tell. Let's start tapping the keys.

~ to ^

SPECIAL USES FOR
diacritics

The tilde (usually placed at medium height, and sometimes called 'bent line' or 'swung dash' in this usage) is used in many dictionaries to stand for the headword: for example, under 'foot, […] *get a ~ in the door; put a ~ wrong; put one's ~ down; put one's ~ in it.*'

The **grave accent** is used in poetry, especially in blank verse, to mark a syllable that is to be pronounced for the sake of the metre. For example, Shakespeare's 'A couch for luxury and damnèd incest' (*Hamlet*, act 1, scene 5).

So are they 'dots' or
'spots' or 'jots'?
Don't be so analytical!
But where you place
those tiny blots,
Is highly diacritical.

add -ons *to the* alphabet

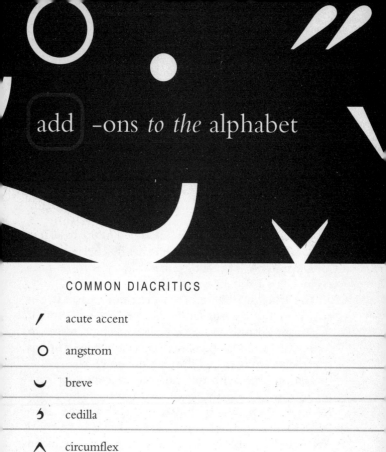

COMMON DIACRITICS

／	acute accent
O	angstrom
◡	breve
ϗ	cedilla
∧	circumflex
•	dot on the *i* [also known as a tittle]
＼	grave accent
∨	háček
–	macron
~	tilde
••	umlaut/diaeresis

SOME SPECIAL USES IN

Pinyin | Chinese

macron used to signify the first tone (*wū* – 'house')
acute accent used to signify the second tone (*wú* – 'none')
háček used to signify the third tone (*wŭ* – 'five')
grave accent used to signify the fourth tone (*wù* – 'fog')

Diacritics are tiny marks that are added to the basic letters of the alphabet. They have many functions, but the most common is to signify that a letter is to be pronounced in a certain way.

The **tilde** is an often-seen diacritical mark. It can attach itself to various letters, but perhaps we know it best from Spanish (*mañana*, where the tilde serves to soften the *n*) and Portuguese (*São Paulo*, where it means that the vowel is voiced through the nose).

The problem with the tilde on the computer keyboard is that it cannot serve its original purpose: you can't type an *n*, then backspace and type a ~ over it to make an *ñ*. To create a *ñ* you have to key it in a special way (see the character chart at the end of this book). So what's the tilde doing on the computer keyboard? To be useful, this tilde must be able to stand alone, without having to rely on another character. Currently, the tilde is applied in some internet addresses, for example, <www.isp.com/~joeblow/myhomepage.htm>, but perhaps better and greater things lie in wait for this curly character.

Another common diacritic is the **umlaut** (which you might think is spelt *ümlaut* in German, but isn't). The umlaut is used by such celebrities as Björn Borg, Hänsel and Gretel, and Baron von Münchhausen.

Those two little dots are of critical — even

diacritical — importance, and forgetting them can be disastrous. Take Swedish, for example, where *skon* means 'the shoe' and *skön* means 'beautiful'. The former is pronounced as in English schooner, the latter sounds something like 'shurn'.

Perhaps because it tends to evoke images of Scandinavia, the umlaut has sometimes been used in product names, presumably to give them a fresh, cool, Nordic flavour. The products might be called *Nörska* or *Mööve* or *Snöwball*, for instance. However, these words are completely meaningless in any Scandinavian language. For unknown reasons, certain rock bands have also adopted the umlaut, such as *Mötörhead*.

When two dots are used to signify that a seemingly silent vowel should be pronounced, this is called a **diæresis** (or dieresis). You might know someone called *Zoë*, for instance, and she might be a *naïve* person from *Güiria*. (She might even be working as a *lingüista*.)

Swedes use the **angstrom** (also known as 'ring above' or 'degree sign') to write *å*, which signifies a sound somewhere between a and o, as in English 'for'.

The **acute** and **grave accents** are familiar to anyone who thinks that tie-dye is *passé* or has chosen a meal from the *à la carte* menu. One mark goes up (the acute) and the other one, easily remembered, goes down (the grave). The accents do not occur in English words, but mainly in French loans, and many people prefer to omit them when writing English. However, the accents do come in handy when you want to distinguish between certain meanings; for instance, if you want to *resume writing* after an interruption, or if you want to get on with your *résumé writing*. And it makes a great difference whether you think someone's dress is pretty lame — or pretty lamé.

The accents are common features of French, as is the **circumflex**, which plays an important rôle in that language. In English it is rarely used, and only in foreign loan-words, such as *maître d'hôtel*.

The **cedilla** is the little hook placed under the letter *c* in order to pronounce it as an *s* as in the word *façade*, which would sound extremely risqué if you pronounced it as a hard *k*. (Try it yourself, then go and wash your mouth.)

The name comes from the Spanish and means 'little z'. This is because the cedilla, before it was attached to the bottom of the *c*, was written as a tiny *z* after the letter. Strangely enough, cedilla is not written *cedilla* or even *çedilla* in Spanish, but *zedilla*.

DIACRITICS HAVE ONE THING IN COMMON
— their subtlety borders on coyness.
None of the diacritics appears in its own description!

The **tilde** is not written tilde
There is no accent in **accent**
The **circumflex** is not written circumflêx
There is no umlaut in **umlaut**
Neither French nor Spanish uses Ç to write **cedilla**
The **macron** is not written măcron
The **breve** is not called brĕve
The **angstrom** should be written Ångström, but isn't

But as always there has to be an exception to the rule:
the **háček**, which indeed is written with a háček.

WHY DIACRITICS?

Although the Romans found that an alphabet of just twenty-one letters was enough for their language, the Latin alphabet was insufficient for many other languages. A simple example is Czech, where there is a difference between short and long vowels. How can you easily make a distinction between a short *a* and a long one?

There are two ways: you either write a double *aa* or add a little mark that signifies 'long', for example *ā* or *á*. Czech, and a lot of other tongues, opted for the diacritic, perhaps for the sake of economy: it took fewer pen strokes and took up less space.

In short, when various language groups adopted the Latin writing system, they added marks to the letters to signify special sounds in their own tongue that could not be described by the simple Latin alphabet.

ABOVE DIACRITICISM

Have you ever looked at the signs outside a Vietnamese restaurant, or seen a Vietnamese newspaper? Even if you don't know a single word of the language, you can recognise the letters, but the writing is laden with diacritical marks.

The Vietnamese language uses Latin script as its basis, but has added a wealth of diacritics to signify lingual features that cannot be conveyed by using the Latin alphabet on its own. This may seem complex and confusing — let alone hard to read — but Vietnamese has nothing on some other languages that are really heavy users of diacritics.

Vietnamese

Western Apache

Aranda (Australia) – before simplification

DO YOU DOT YOUR *i*'S?

The dot on the *i* (and the *j*, which is originally the same letter) is the single diacritic used in English. It often goes by the name 'tittle'.

Why do we place a dot on the *i*?

It has to do with something called 'minim confusion'.

In handwriting, a minim is the small downward stroke used in *m, n, i, u,* and so on. In early writing there was no dot on the *i*, and the minims were written almost identically. This could lead to confusion in words containing a lot of minims next to each other This sequence of only three minims, for instance, could read *in, iu, m, ni,* or *ui.*

Try writing the word 'minimum' in your own cursive hand without dotting the *i*'s.

Depending on your handwriting, the result is often quite confusing.

The dot on the *i* (which at first looked like an acute accent) was first added by a scribe in the Middle English period who had an *i* for clarity and a desire to make a point.

PUNCTUATION

! to ?

Many writers profess great exactness in punctuation, who never yet made a point.

GEORGE
DENNISON
PRENTICE

DOT, JOT, DASH OR SLASH — WHAT'S THE POINT?

The eccentric (and self-anointed) Lord Timothy Dexter didn't see any point in punctuation: in 1802 he wrote a book called *A Pickle for the Knowing Ones*, which was completely devoid of punctuation (it was also lacking in capitalisation, correct spelling, rules of grammar and general readability). When readers complained, the good Lord added a single page to the second edition, filled with a profusion of commas, colons, stops and other signs, so that his readers could 'pepper and salt' his book with punctuation marks to their hearts' content.

The Lord wrote:

fourder mister printer the Nowing ones complane of my book the fust edition had no stops I put in A nuf here and thay may peper and solt it as they please

What is the role of punctuation? Its importance can be easily demonstrated by stripping a passage of text of its punctuation marks — such as this one from *The Jolly Corner* by Henry James.

The great thing to see she presently said seems to me to be that it has spoiled nothing it hasn't spoiled your being here at last it hasn't spoiled this it hasn't spoiled your speaking she also however faltered he wondered at everything her controlled emotion might mean do you believe then too dreadfully that I am as good as I might ever have been oh no far from it with which she got up from her chair and was nearer to him but I don't care she smiled

After a while, you lose track. When we put back the punctuation marks, the text suddenly becomes meaningful and readable.

'The great thing to see,' she presently said, 'seems to me to be that it has spoiled nothing. It hasn't spoiled your being here at last. It hasn't spoiled this. It hasn't spoiled your speaking —' She also however faltered.

He wondered at everything her controlled emotion might mean. 'Do you believe then — too dreadfully! — that I am as good as I might ever have been?'

'Oh, no! Far from it!' With which she got up from her chair and was nearer to him. 'But I don't care,' she smiled.

The punctuation marks we sprinkle into our writing are mere youngsters compared to the letters of the alphabet.

Early writing did not make use of punctuation marks as we know them. No full stops in this period!

There were two major reasons for this lack of punctuation. Firstly, authors usually dictated their thoughts to a scribe, and we don't use punctuation marks in speech. The scribe's job was to take down the spoken words (and nothing else) as accurately and quickly as possible. Secondly, all writing was intended for reading aloud. Writing was all about speaking: silent reading was unheard of.

In early Latin manuscripts small dots called *interpuncts* were used to separate words. This practice was probably inherited from the Etruscans. However, by AD 100 it had all but died out. Texts from this time and for many centuries to follow were written in a continuous string withoutspacesbetweenthewords (see 'Space' in the section 'Punctuation marks and symbols on the keyboard and beyond').

There was very little to assist the reader: the only hint was that major sections sometimes were out-dented, that is, the first line of a new distinct part projected into the left margin, and was begun with an initial letter that was slightly larger than the rest of the text.

The only mark used by the scribe was in the form of a *K* (for *Kaput*, 'head') written at the beginning or 'head' of a rhetorical argument. The K was later replaced by a *C* (for *capitulum*, 'chapter') and became a punctuation mark which is, although very familiar to computer users, rarely actually used by anyone nowadays (see ¶ in the section 'Punctuation marks and symbols on the keyboard and beyond').

After taking down the author's dictation, the scribe would pass on the manuscript to a teacher, whose duty was to prepare the text for reading aloud. This meant doing two things: short oblique strokes called *apices* were added above certain vowels to guide the reader's intonation; long strokes would signify pauses and guide the reader's rhythm.

In addition, a mark called *paragraphus* Γ might be inserted to mark distinct sections of the text. The sign was derived from the Greek letter *gamma* Γ, and could also be written as a lower-case *gamma* γ. Why *gamma*? It was a case of G for 'text': in Greek, *para-* means 'beside', and *graphos* means 'text'.

The *hedera* or ivy-leaf was used to signify the end of a text. This is one of the oldest punctuation marks, in use since around 200 BC.

The *scriptura continua* (lack of word spaces) was a great nuisance for readers, and mistakes were common. Manuscripts from the period tell of the difficulties, and give several examples of amusing and embarrassing errors made in the reading of texts.

An example in English might serve to illustrate the problem. What would you make of the following text?

ANDSOAKINGWASHEVERYTHINGAUNT

And so, a king was he: very thin, gaunt.
And soaking! Wash everything, Aunt!

THE FIRST DOTS APPEAR

In the 5th and 6th centuries, a system of dots called *distinctiones* was implemented. It had first been invented (but was a flop) by Aristophanes of Byzantium, who was the librarian of the library at Alexandria in 200 BC.

Aristophanes had invented three marks, which he called *comma*, *colon* and *periodos*. Although their names sound like punctuation marks, they were initially used to divide a statement into its logical parts: its premises, arguments, conclusions, and so on.

It worked like this in Latin texts: a single dot was inserted at different positions in the text to tell the speaker (silent reading was unknown, or at least a rarity on a par with magic) where to make a short, medium or long pause. A dot on the baseline marked a minor pause. At medium height the dot had the function of our colon: it signified a division between two complete senses but incomplete meanings. And a dot at the top of a letter meant a final pause after a complete meaning, like our full stop.

Here is an example in English.

TO WIT. THE MARKS WERE THREE • AND WRIT FOR ALL TO SEE •

Aristophanes's dots disappeared in Latin when the Romans started to write all words butted together without any word separations. The marks did, however, reappear a few hundred years later.

SIMPLEX ... AND NOT SO SIMPLEX

The Irish monks who invented the word-space in the second half of the first millennium of the Christian era invented a number of abbreviations and signs, too, which they inserted in the text. They also started to use a mark that looked like a small number seven 7 which they inserted to mark a brief medial pause. This was known as a *simplex ductus*. Sometimes the 'seven' was doubled or even tripled to mark a slightly longer pause.

AT THE POINT OF MADNESS

By AD 1000 scribes had become positively dotty about punctuation.

European manuscripts were strewn with all sorts of marks: the system had become extremely rich, varied, arbitrary and confusing, if not chaotic.

Until the 7th and 8th centuries, there had been no lower-case letters. The low-middle-high *distinctiones* dots were easy to see alongside the CAPITALS. But the introduction of Carolingian lower-case letters meant that some lines (called *ascenders*) projected above the body of the letters (like *d*) and some (called *descenders*) projected below the baseline (like *p*). The *distinctiones* dots became hard to work out: it was now hard to see what was 'bottom', 'middle' and 'top'.

Another punctuation system slowly came into existence: the marks were called *positurae* and were used in addition to all the other marks. At first, the new system comprised four distinct marks.

Punctus [circum]flexus ⌐

Punctus elevatus ⸫

Punctus interrogativus ⸮ or ⸯ

Punctus versus ⁊ or ⸵

All of these were used in various places, depending on the context, the type of phrase, the sense of the clause and the meaning of the whole statement. You can tell by their shape that they were chiefly inflexional signs, drawing a picture of the pitch of the voice as a guide for reading aloud.

The new system was used in conjunction with all the older marks. So, the low-middle-high *distinctiones* dots were still in use, as was the *K*, which often was written .*K*. with a dot on either side. The virgule / was another popular sign, used to denote a short break. The Irish *simplex ductus* was also in use, and different dots and comma-like signs were all over the place: the more dots, the more important the segment, and the longer the pause. For instance —

⠸   was used for a minor pause

⸫, or ⸪,   was used for a final pause.

In other words, punctuation had become a terrible mess, and it got still worse. After AD 1000 it was almost impossible to choose which mark to use — but still more kept coming. For example, if the virgule / was used for a brief pause, the ⸰ did the job of a longer one. But this was not enough for some scribes: they devised a ⫽ for something in between.

In the 1200s many scribes had had enough of the confusion and thought that it was pointless to continue with it. It was time to start to Keep It Simple Stupid. Some began to use only two punctuation marks: one virgule / (the old *virgula suspensiva*) for minor pauses, and another virgule — (*virgula plana*) for major ones.

This was far too simplistic for other scribes. The result, towards the 14th century, was something of a compromise. The art of writing became more stabilised and certain writing conventions began to form.

Then, in the mid 1400s, along came Johannes Gutenberg and his wonderful moveable-type printing press, which marked the birth of typography and mass-produced books. This development further served to put a stop to chaotic punctuation. The venerated Venetian printer Aldus Manutius (also known as Aldo Manuzio il Vecchio or Teobaldo Manucci) set up a printing house specialising in excellently edited, low-cost pocket books. His grandson, of the same name, continued to make a great impression on the writing of the time, and was the first to construct a sensible, regulated punctuation system. In 1566 he published a book entitled *Orthographiae ratio* ('System of Orthography'), which contained the comma, colon, semi-colon and full stop.

Many modern punctuation marks were born in this period, such as the question mark (stemming from the old *punctus interrogativus*) and, much later, the exclamation mark. The semi-colon became very popular towards the end of the 1400s. The earlier signs all had to do with reading aloud: how long to pause, when to breathe, when to raise the pitch of your voice, and so on. The new generation of punctuation marks (such as parentheses) clearly reflected the fact that silent reading had become a part of life. In other words, the role of the punctuation mark changed from an inflexional 'musical' one to a syntactical 'meaningful' one.

@ to &

SIMPLE SYMBOLS

A symbol is something that represents something else. & is a good example of a symbol: it stands for 'and'. @ represents the word 'at', but also the notion of 'this much [product] in exchange for that much [money]'. In addition, it signifies the connection between an email user's name and the worldwide web domain where that name resides.

However, symbols do not have to be signs with swirls and curlicues. Take the letter x which can be used as a symbol — to represent a kiss; or to stand for something or someone unknown, for instance, as in 'Mister X'. The chemical symbol Au stands for gold.

Some symbols lead a double life, acting as both punctuation

marks and symbols, as is the case with the closing quotation mark ” which doubles as the symbol for 'ditto' in lists.

Many of our symbols have one feature in common: they are all single letters or pairs of letters that have had a line drawn through them or added above or under them, such as £ ¢ N°. The line alerts the reader that this is not an *L* or *c* or No — this is a symbol representing something else.

While *X* is an abstract concept, the symbols for pound (sterling), cent, and number (above) are, like most symbols on the keyboard, abbreviations of words. This was done either by *suspension* (cutting off the end of the word) or *contraction* (omitting the middle of the word). Thus, the symbols above stand for 'L[ī̄bra pondō]', 'c[entum]', and 'N[umer]o', respectively.

In fact, nearly all the symbols on and off the keyboard — even # and % and @ — have evolved from a letter and a line; invented by writers to save s p a c e, TIME, **ink**, *effort*, and perhaps ~~writing cramp~~.

Some abbreviations we still use today may be encountered with or without the little line, such as the abbreviations for the ordinal numbers. 1st 2nd 3rd

Abbreviations became very popular in medieval times. Apart from making shortcuts for frequently used words for the sake of timesaving, scribes also shortened sacred or revered names as a sign of reverence (it was a common Jewish tradition to show veneration by not spelling out God's name in full, for instance), and texts are full of abbreviations such as for Christus (*Xp* is the Greek letter sequence for 'Chr').

𝕏𝕡𝕦𝕤

However work-saving, these shortcuts came at a price: by the end of the Middle Ages, the number of abbreviations had reached at least 13,000.

0 1 2 3 4 5 6 7 8 9

$$0 \text{ to } 9$$

NUMERO UNO, AND THEN SOME
Just above the sprawl of QWERTY letters on your keyboard you'll find a row of characters that have nothing to do with letters. Most keyboards have another set of exactly the same characters on the 'numeric keypad' on the right-hand side of the keyboard. Something that appears twice on a tiny keyboard where space is at a premium has to be important.

We're talking numbers.

Anything from

$$1 + 1 = 2$$

to the number of stars in the universe. Like the

twenty-six letter-keys making words that can describe the world, those ten number keys can quantify everything in it.

ROMAN NUMERALS

How do you write zero in Roman numerals?
You can't.

The Romans could count from one to ten and use numbers in their thousands, but they couldn't count to zero. Like many other number systems, Roman numerals simply do not feature a character that means nothing.

In Roman times counting was done as a 'tally plan', just like notches on the wall of a prisoner's cell.

The V for five and X for ten were simply graphic shortcuts in the tally system, and it is easy to see why.

The subtraction system of, say, IV for four (instead of IIII) and IX for nine (instead of VIIII) was not Roman at all: it was invented about a thousand years after the end of the Roman period.

Larger numbers were derived from the Etruscans, as you can see from the following table.

Number	Etruscan	Roman
50	V	V ⇒ ⊥ ⇒ L
100	⊗	⊙ ⇒ O ⇒ C
1000	Φ	CIƆ ⇒ ⊂IƆ ⇒ ⊂Ɔ ⇒ M
500 is simply 'half a thousand'		IƆ OR D

Even greater numbers can be written in two ways.

5000	$\overline{V}$	or $IƆƆ$
10,000	$\overline{X}$	or $CCIƆƆ$
50,000	$\overline{L}$	or $IƆƆƆ$
100,000	$\overline{C}$	or $CCCIƆƆƆ$
500,000	$\overline{D}$	or $IƆƆƆƆ$
1,000,000	$\overline{M}$	or $CCCCIƆƆƆƆ$

The line above a numeral means 'multiple of 1000', and is a convenient way of writing large numbers. Thus, 490,000 can simply be written $\overline{XD}$.

ARABIC NUMERALS

We call them 'Arabic numerals'. But they're not Arabic. The Arabs called them 'Persian numerals'. But they're not Persian. The Persians called them 'Hindu numerals'. And indeed they are.

Hindu scholars invented the first version of our number system. Unfortunately, the scholars wrote using a stylus on dried palm leaves, which means that none of their work has survived. Palaeographers have worked backwards from our modern numbers through findings of later written numbers from archaeological sites, and arrived at a 'conjectured' series of what the earliest Hindu numbers might have looked like.

The idea was to write a digit using as many strokes as the number it signified. The number 1 would have one stroke, number 2 would require two strokes, and so on.

There was one additional requirement: the numbers had to be written with straight lines. Writing on brittle palm leaves was much easier if you used straight lines:

writing curved shapes with the stylus often resulted in the leaf splitting

The development of the 'Arabic' numerals from the conjectured Hindu scholars' straight-lined stroke-counts to our modern number shapes is shown below.

'Conjectured'

Early Persian (designed for easier continuous writing)

Gobar numbers (Arabic word meaning 'dust' — possibly characters being written in sand sprinkled on a pupil's slate)

European printer's font (1478)

Modern

1 2 3 4 5 6 7 8 9 0

An Italian mathematician, Leonardo Fibonacci (or Leonardo Pisano), was instrumental in bringing the Indian/Arabic system to Europe. He spent years travelling around North Africa studying different methods of calculation.

In 1202 he wrote a work called *Liber Abaci* ('Book of the Abacus'), in which he spent seven chapters explaining that zero as a number was a very useful thing, and then demonstrated how easily calculations could be done by using the Indian/Arabic system in business, trade, money-changing, weight-conversion, profit margin, and many other practical fields.

These calculations would have been impossible using Roman numerals

$$\frac{\begin{array}{r} \text{MDCLXVIII} \\ \div \ \text{IV} \end{array}}{= \text{CDXVII}}$$

**MODERN-DAY
TALLY PLAN**

If you ever go to a Chinese *yum cha* restaurant, you may well see a different kind of tally plan on your tab.

一 丁 下 丏 正

As you order dishes, the waiter may jot down one line for each order on your tab. After five orders, the final result will be the Chinese character for 'correct'.

ZILCH

The Arabic word for 'nil' or 'empty' was (and still is) *sifr*. Fibonacci called it *zephirum* in his native Italian. Two centuries later, it was called *zeuero*, and that's how English got its word for nothing at all: zero.

Perhaps because a number standing for nothing was an entirely mysterious concept to Europeans, English got another word from the same Arabic *sifr*: cipher.

COUNT LIKE AN EGYPTIAN

The Egyptians had special hieroglyphs for numbers; even very large numbers. But, like the Romans, they had no notion of zero as a number.

All the hieroglyphic numerals were used in the tally-plan fashion.

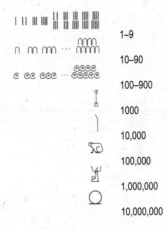

1–9

10–90

100–900

1000

10,000

100,000

1,000,000

10,000,000

Letters

K E Y B

Q to M

on the

O A R D

℞   ℬ

℗

𝔜

𝔏 𝔭 ℌ   𝔍

𝔶

SPECIAL USES FOR Q

Q and **q** as abbreviations
stand for: heat, quart, quarter,
quarterly, quartermaster,
quarto, Quebec, queen,
queen (in chess), query, question,
quintal, quire

PARTRIDGE'S
COMIC
ALPHABETS

Q for flowers
*(Kew [Gardens]
for flowers)*

57

No-one knows with certainty the exact meaning of *Q*. It came from a sign that looked like this ϙ.

By about 1000 BC it had changed to a much more *Q*-like letter ϙ.

Researchers have argued about *Q* for a long time. The explanations for its shape that have been presented span an amazing range: the vulva of a cow, a pestle, a face looking forward, a club or a baton, a sandal thong or the heart and trachea.

What we know is that the ancient Greeks took the character on board, called it *koppa*, and then summarily dumped it. They had no use for *Q*, and in Classical Greek it is completely missing.

The Etruscans rescued it, though. They wrote it in several different ways, but two of them would become our modern lower-case *q* and upper-case *Q* Ρ ϙ.

The reason why *Q* is never used in English unless it is followed by a *U* dates back to the Etruscans. They had three ways of writing the 'k' sound: *K*, *C*, and *Q*. The *Q* was used exclusively before the 'u' sound.

LOWER-CASE *q*

Our lower-case *q* looks very different from the upper-case *Q*. This is because the rounder of the two Etruscan versions came to be used in Roman lapidary style (monumental characters chiselled into stone), and the other version was used in the Roman cursive style (for writing with a pen or brush on papyrus).

Etruscan; Etruscan (reversed); Roman cursive; modern

looking for
W
go to F

e

SPECIAL USES FOR E

E and **e** as abbreviations
stand for: earl, earth, east, ecstasy
(the drug — slang), Egyptian,
electric field strength,
electromotive force, electron,
energy, engineering,
English, Erlang, Spain
(international car registration)

PARTRIDGE'S
COMIC
ALPHABETS

E for brick
(heave a brick)

The letter *E* comes from a picture of a praying man, dating back to about 1500 BC ⌐ᴴ⌐.

The praying fellow gradually became legless ⌐ᴵᴱᴵ⌐ and, after a while, he lost his head as well! ⌐ᴸᴸ⌐.

Around the year 1000 BC, the Phoenicians found that it suited their right-to-left writing to turn the *E* around to 'face' left. They also placed a little tail at the bottom of the *E* ∃.

The tail grew and the *E* started to lean even further leftward ⋛.

Like all other vowels, *E* started off as a consonant. Its name was *heh*. The Greeks, finding that they had no use for *heh* but needed a vowel *e*, named it *epsilon*.

The Greeks, writing in their boustrophedon to-and-fro style, mirror-reversed the *E*, according to the direction of writing. By the 5th century BC, the left-to-right writing was established, the *E* lost its tail and was stabilised as the *E* we know. The letter, ready-made, slipped effortlessly into the Etruscan and Latin alphabets without any major modifications.

LOWER-CASE e

Capital *E* has four strokes: three horizontal ones and one vertical. The Roman stonemasons didn't care about the number of strokes: chiselling the letters into stone, they were only concerned about straight lines. *E* was a cinch.

But people using a pen or brush found an alternative way of writing *E* that was much faster, using just two strokes, yet looking sufficiently like the monumental *E* ⨍.

Later on, in the half-uncial style, the horizontal line almost became the main feature of the letter ℮.

This is the basis for our modern ℮, often simplified to a single-stroke ℓ.

SPECIAL USES FOR R

R and **r** as abbreviations stand for: rabbi, radical, radius, railway, rand, rare, recipe, recto, rector, regiment, regina, registered trademark (usually written as the ® symbol), Republican (US), resistance, response, restricted (as in R-rated), rex, right, river, road, rod, roentgen, Romania (international car registration), rook (chess), rouble, royal, ruled, run, rupee

PARTRIDGE'S
COMIC
ALPHABETS

R for moment
(half a moment)

61

The letter *R* stems from the hieroglyph depicting a human head in profile 𓀮.

In North Semitic the head and neck were simplified 𓀮, then stylised and written like a back-to-front *P* 𓀮.

When the Greeks started writing from left to right, the letter they had imported, which they called *rho*, looked like the Latin *P*. This was not a problem for the Greeks, because they had modified their *P* to the square-shaped Π. There was no mistaking *P* for Π.

Some Greek writers, however, had written *P* in a different form, using an angular 'leg' of the *P* rather than a vertical one 𓀮. Yet others wrote it as 𓀮. These later forms were the precursors of our Latin *R*.

LOWER-CASE *r*

When writing with a chisel on stone, the Romans used the monumental form *R*. When writing with pen or brush on papyrus, they wrote in a simpler, more flowing style. There was more than one way of writing the character 𓀮𓀮. This became our lower-case *r*.

SPECIAL USES FOR T

Used to describe things shaped like a T, such as T-square, T-bar, T-junction, T-bone.

Also found in the phrase 'to a T'. This probably comes from the 14th century expression 'to a tittle'. A tittle is a tiny point or dot in writing, such as the dot on the *i*.

T and **t** as abbreviations stand for: absolute temperature, distribution, surface tension, tare, teaspoonful, temperature, tempo, *tempore*, tenor, tense, tera-, territory, tesla, Thailand (international car registration), time, ton, tonne, trainer (aircraft), transitive, tritium, troy, Tuesday

Do you cross your *T*s? Of course not. But you do cross your *t*s.

The *T* used to look like an *X* or a cross ✕ ✝.

It used to reside on top of the heart in an Egyptian hieroglyph meaning 'heart and trachea' ⚱.

In modern Hebrew, the letter is called *tav*, which means 'mark' or 'sign'. This makes you wonder whether the little *x*, placed where you're supposed to sign on the bottom line, is really an *x* meaning unknown, or a *T*, meaning 'sign'.

The Greeks imported the character as ✝ , and then lopped the top off to create ⊤.

The letter was adopted by the Etruscans and then passed into Latin without change. The lower-case *t*, however, retained the top of the cross, and that is why you cross your *t*s but not your *T*s.

IJY

looking for
U
go to F

ijy

SPECIAL USES FOR IJY

As abbreviations these letters stand for:

I and **i** — 1 (Roman numerals), current, incisor, independence, institute, interest, international, intransitive, Iodine, island, isle, isospin, Italy (international car registration)

J and **j** — jack, Japan (international car registration), joule, journal, judge, justice

Y and **y** — year, yen, yttrium, yuan

PARTRIDGE'S
COMIC
ALPHABETS

I for an eye
(eye for an eye)
J for oranges
(Jaffa oranges)
Y for mistress
(wife or mistress)

I, J and Y all stem from one Egyptian hieroglyph depicting a forearm and hand ⌐⌐▢ .

In Semitic languages *yod* corresponds to the word for 'hand'.

This character was used extensively in Egyptian. If a piece of bread was put in the

> The *I* we use to denote 'me' dates from the 12th century: in Old English, I was called *ic*, and in Old Saxon *ik*. (Compare German *ich*.)
>
> Y is one of the few letters of the English alphabet whose name is not pronounced as the sound it makes.

hand, the character meant 'offering' or 'gift'. If the hand was turned downward, the sign meant 'stop'. The notion of negation was expressed by two arms barring the way ⌐⌐⌐ . And it wasn't difficult to write the sign for 'hug' or 'embrace' ⌒⌒ .

The Phoenicians simplified the hand and arm a little and turned it 90 degrees ⌐ .

When the Greeks imported ⌐ *yod*, it had developed somewhat and looked something like ⌐ . It lost its 'thumb' and was mirror-reversed ⌐ . This was not very different from the letter for *sigma* ⌐ and could easily be confused. The letter took on a more upright ⌐ stance and later became our *I*.

From the Semitic *yod*, the Greeks called the letter *iota*. Iota was just a jot. It was surely the skinniest and plainest letter in the alphabet: a single short stroke of the pen. This is why you say that you don't care an iota, or you don't give a jot.

(But the jot didn't have a dot. For an explanation why we place a dot (the proper name is 'tittle') on the lower-case *i*, see the section 'Diacritics: add-ons to the alphabet'.)

Y AND J

Y is a younger kind of *I* and dates from around 50 BC. It stems from the same Egyptian forearm.

J was a much later invention, dating from only five hundred years ago, on an initiative from Peter Ramus.

It was designed to differentiate between the Latin vowel *I* and the consonant *I*, both of which were pronounced the same way.

Confused? So were the Romans. When *I* was standing proud between two consonants, *I* was a vowel, as in VINO. But often when *I* was placed before or after another vowel, I became a consonant, as in IESU for Jesus.

The name Jesus, using the letter *J*, is a mediaeval corruption of the original name, which was Yeshu (or Ieshu), which in turn was a contraction of the name Yehoshua (modern Joshua).

The shape of the letter *j* may have come from the practice of adding a little tail to the final *i* if a Latin word ended in *ii*, for instance, *filii* became *filij*. The same applied to Roman numerals in lower case: xiii became xiij. This convention can still be seen in the Dutch language: what used to be written *miine* ('mine') became *mijne*, and is still written that way.

English printers started differentiating between *j* and *i* around 1630. As late as 1813, American dictionaries still placed words like 'jam', 'job' and 'jug' under the same heading as 'ice', 'ill' and 'ink'.

WHY AM I NOT I?

The practice of writing an upper-case *I* for the first person pronoun dates back to about AD 1250 and has to do with legibility. *I* used to be called *ic* in Old English, but in unstressed positions it became *i* which was easily misread and confused with neighbouring words. Rendering *i* a capital *I* made it a distinct word and solved the problem. In the south of England, where *ic* was called *ich*, I took another 500 years to take hold.

SPECIAL USES FOR O

O is often used to signify the shape of a circle: O-ring, O-shape, and so on.

O and o as abbreviations stand for: nought, ocean, octavo, old, only, order, oxygen, pint

The hieroglyph that became the letter O was a picture of an eye. 👁 The hieroglyph on its own meant 'to do' or 'to enable'.

In the North Semitic alphabet the pupil shrank to a simple dot at first. 👁 Later the eye itself became more rounded. ☉ The Greeks adopted the letter as *omicron* (not *omega*) and, later, the eye of the O lost its dot.

PARTRIDGE'S
COMIC
ALPHABETS

O for the rainbow
(over the rainbow)

68

P

SPECIAL USES FOR
P

P and **p** as abbreviations stand for: momentum, page, parity, parking, part, participle, past, pastor, pataca, pawn, pence, per, peseta, peso, pharmacy only, phosphorus, piano, pico-, pint, pipe, poise, population, Portugal (international car registration), post, power, president, pressure, priest, prince, pro, proton, pula

p

PARTRIDGE'S
COMIC
ALPHABETS

P for relief
(pee for relief)

The letter *P* comes from the hieroglyph meaning 'mouth' ⬭.

Peh means 'mouth' in some modern Semitic tongues, such as Hebrew.

However, the *P* ⬭ was easily confused with the character for *O* ⬭ (the eye) — only a single dot made all the difference. So the character was modified to a long rectangle that still could be construed as a mouth ▭.

What happened next is a bit of a mystery. It seems that the mouth began to smile ∨.

Those curves were joined, and by 1000 BC the letter *P* looked like an upside-down J ⌐.

The Greeks took on the letter, called it *pi*, and wrote it in two ways — either with a round 'crook' or a square one ⌐ Γ. After a while, they seemed to prefer the squared-off variant, and applied their sense of symmetry to make both legs equally long. The character became *pi* as we know it Π.

The Latin alphabet, however, adopted the version with the rounded 'crook' and closed up the head. The result was our familiar letter *P*.

A

SPECIAL USES FOR A

A is often used to signify 'excellence', as in 'grade A' and 'A-class' and 'A1', but can also mean something bad, as in 'to give someone the big A', where *A* stands for 'Arse'.

A and **a** as abbreviations stand for: acreage, alto, amateur, ampere, answer, area, atom (as in A-bomb), Austria (international car registration)

a

PARTRIDGE'S
COMIC
ALPHABETS

A for 'orses
(hay for horses)

A has always been the first letter of our alphabet. It is also the first letter of the ancient Greek, Arabic and Hebrew, and many other alphabets. The very word 'alphabet' comes from the Semitic and Greek names for the first two letters *A* and *B*:

alif, ba	ARABIC
alef, beth	HEBREW
alpha, beta	GREEK

The origin of the letter *A* is a 5000-year old Egyptian hieroglyphic meaning 'ox'. It was a picture of the head of an ox and looked like this.

So what has the letter *A* got to do with a portrait of an ox? To see the connection, you'll have to turn the *A* upside down, paint in the eyes and use a little imagination to see the head, the horns and the ears.

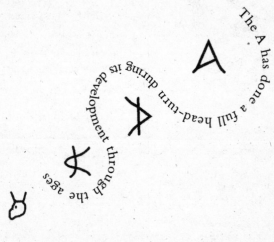

The A has done a full head-turn during its development through the ages

LOWER-CASE *a*

Why does the lower-case *a* look so different from the upper-case *A*? The lower-case letters did not appear until the late 700s, but the Romans had several ways of writing their letters. For carving the letters in marble, for instance, they used the capitals we know as Roman capitals today (*A*, for instance). When they wrote with a pen on papyrus, however, they used simplified characters called 'cursive capitals' (second from the top in the picture below). These cursives would later form the basis of our lower-case letters.

Greek

Roman cursive

uncial

Carolingian

modern

SPECIAL USES FOR S

S and **s** as abbreviations stand for: entropy, fellow (for *socius*, in titles), Sabbath, saint, satisfactory, Saturday, Saxon, schilling, school, sea, second, section, see, semi-, senate, September, siemens, sign(ed), signor, singular, sire, small, socialist, society, sol, son, south, substantive, succeeded, sucre, sulphur, Sunday, Sweden (international car registration)

S

PARTRIDGE'S
COMIC
ALPHABETS

S for instance
(as for instance)

74

Although it looks like a slithering serpent, the *S* does not come from the hieroglyph for 'snake' (that honour belongs to *N*). In fact, the hieroglyphic origins of *S* are even more mysterious than those of the letter *Q*.

Some say that the origin of the letter *S* is a picture of a tooth (*shin*, which is the name for the letter in Hebrew and Arabic, means 'tooth'). Others claim it is a weapon similar to a bow. A lotus pond is also a common explanation. The stylised North Semitic character looked like this. After a while, the ends curled inwards.

Later, about the time it was adopted by the Greeks, the letter *S* had become more angular and had been turned on its end. When the Greeks started writing from left to right, the little wiggle was squared up and became the familiar *sigma* Σ.

Some writers dropped one of the 'legs', and others wrote it in a rounded curve instead of the angular strokes. It is easy to see how this twirl ended up as our *S*.

LOWER-CASE s

The modern lower-case *s* is just a small version of the upper-case *S*. But if you study older texts, you will notice that *s* often resembles the letter *f*. This may be quite difficult to read, especially if a sentence contains a lot of *f*s as well as a lot of *s*'s. A sentence might look as follows at first glance.

At firſt, Uncle Feſter's buſineſs ſuffered in the moſt unforeſeen faſhion.

But if you look at it closely, it becomes much clearer.

At firſt, Uncle Feſter's buſineſs ſuffered in the moſt unforeſeen faſhion.

What a difference! Look closely at the characters that look like *f*s: Some have a cross-bar. Those are *f*s. And some have a little bar at the left that does NOT cross the character. Those are *s*'s.

If *s* was at the end of a word, it was written as our modern lower-case *s*. This meant that a word like 'senselessness' was written

ſenſeleſſneſs.

And senseless it was, because it was hard *to read*.

This last double-*s* combination of a 'tall *s*' and a 'short *s*' was later combined into a single ligature (binding together of two letters), which is still in common use in the German double-*s*, variously known as *ess-tzett* or *es-tzet* or *scharfes S* ß . Note that this character has nothing to do with the Greek character *beta* (β).

Where did these twin formations come from? The Romans, of course. While the monumental stone-cutting fashion was always in the shape of an *S*, the cursive way of writing ſʏ ſ with a pen or brush was often different.

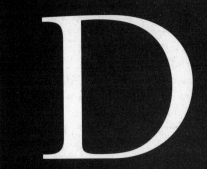

SPECIAL USES FOR D

D and **d** as abbreviations stand for: 500 (Roman numerals), dam, date, daughter, day, degree, delete, Democrat (US), depart, department, deuterium, diameter, died, dinar, diopter, director, dispersion, dollar, Don (Spanish title), dose, drachma, drag, Dutch, duchess, duke, Germany (international car registration), penny (British).

PARTRIDGE'S
COMIC
ALPHABETS

D for rent
(different)

The origin of the letter *D* is a disputed matter. Fish, door, or breast? Those are the main contestants.

Some claim that it is a fish, either its tail fins or its head ⊲. Others think it is a door. The Egyptian hieroglyph for 'door' looked like this ▯. Yet others believe that the *D* is simply a woman's breast. In Egyptian, this could be represented in various ways ▽◡▽.

fish	=	*dag*
door	=	*dalet*
breast	=	*dad*

The problem is that these three words all start with the '*d*' sound and are thus acrophonic.

It is tempting to favour the 'door' hypothesis because of the convenient similarity between *dalet* and the Greek *delta*. On the other hand, the woman's breast cannot be discounted, not the least because the North Semitic alphabet has several other letters that are based on parts of the human body (see *I, K, O, P, R, S*).

Whatever the original meaning of *D*, it soon became a simple triangle pointing either left or right, depending on which direction you happened to write ◁.

When the Greeks adopted it, they decided to stand the triangle on a solid base with the point upwards Δ. This was the *delta* as we know it.

The Etruscans did not set the triangle on its base: they still used it in the Phoenician way, pointing either left or right. Soon, the letter again acquired the rounded shape it used to have when it was a hieroglyph.

The Romans, writing from left to right, turned the character around and it became the familiar *D*.

LOWER-CASE *d*

We write our modern upper-case *D* in the Roman way, and our lower-case *d* in the Etruscan manner. The Romans themselves had only CAPITAL letters, but several versions. The right-pointing *D* was used for chiselling the letter into marble and stone. When they wrote with a pen on papyrus, the Romans used a cursive style in various shapes based on the left-pointing Etruscan original ↄ ↄ .

SPECIAL USES FOR **FUVW**

F is a four-letter word: *F* or eff can stand for 'fuck', as in 'F off, will you!?'; 'he went effing mad'. 'Sweet F.A.' stands for a presumably good-natured person called Fanny Adams, whose name in turn stands for something not so sweet.

U is a Burmese title of respect for a man: U Thant.

W is written as a double-*V*, but its name is double-*U*. This has to do with *U* and *V* originally being the same letter. **W** is one of the few letters of the English alphabet whose name is not pronounced as the sound it makes.

PARTRIDGE'S
COMIC
ALPHABETS

F for vest
(effervesced)
U for nerve
(you've a nerve!)
V for l'amour
(vive l'amour)
W for a shilling
(double you for a shilling)

As abbreviations these letters stand for:

F and **f** — Fahrenheit, farad, fathom, Fellow, female, feminine, fighter, filly, fine, florin, fluorine, folio, following, force, forte, foul, franc, France (international car registration), frequency, function

U and **u** — union, united, university, upper class, uranium, Uruguay (international car registration)

V and **v** — 5 (Roman numerals), luminous efficiency, vanadium, Vatican City (international car registration), velocity, venerable, ventral, verb, verse, version, verso, versus, very, victory, *vide* (Latin: see), violin, viscount, volt, volume, vocative, voice, volume, von

W and **w** — tungsten, Wales, warden, watt, Wednesday, weekly, weight, Welsh, west, western, wide, width, widow, widower, wife, with, wolfram, women's size, work.

F started its life as a peg. It looked like this ႒ .

A little blob on a stick seems a humble beginning, but this little character would develop not only into *F*, but into *U*, *V*, and *W*. Some experts believe that it was the origin of the Latin *Y* as well.

Its name was *vav*, which even in modern Hebrew means 'peg', and was pronounced as a voiced 'v', not a voiceless 'f'.

The little ring on top opened up, rendering the letter reminiscent of a *Y* or an upside-down *h*.

The transition to Greek saw the two 'horns' at the top folding over to the left. They then began to droop downwards. The lower 'horn' then drifted down the vertical pole until it was parallel with the upper stroke.

This letter, still pronounced 'v', was called *vau* or *digamma* in Greek. It later disappeared in the Classical Greek alphabet, simply because the 'v' sound does not occur in Greek, and there was already a letter for the 'f' sound in *phi*.

CONFUSION

When the Etruscans adopted *F*, it was pronounced as a bilabial 'v', that is, not with the lower lip against the upper teeth, but with both lips loosely together like in Spanish 'b' (as in *Habana*).

The problem was that the Etruscans did have an 'f' sound, but no letter to signify it. At first they combined *v* with *h*, and wrote *vh* to denote *F*.

In the original Latin, *V* was used for both the consonant *v* and the vowel *u* (this interchangeability is often seen even today, such as a boutique called FORVM ROMANVM).

The English language did not differentiate between *V* and *U* until the mid-1600s, when they started to write EVERY and SERVE instead of EUERY and SERUE.

In German the 'f' sound is represented by the letter *V* (called *fau* in German), and the 'v' sound is written *W* (*ve*). Thus, we get *voll* (pronounced with an 'f') for full, but *woll*- (pronounced with a 'v') for wool.

SUMMARY

It is likely that the Greeks imported the Υ Ч character twice: once in about 1100 BC to make *F* (*vau* or *digamma*), and then again around 1000 BC to make an *ypsilon* or *upsilon* (a letter that looks like a *Y*), which was the Greek letter for *U*.

The ypsilon was adopted into the Latin script as *V*, and stood for both the consonant *V* and the vowel *U*.

U as we know it, however, was not invented until the Middle Ages. It was created as a variant of the interchangeable *V* and to get rid of the confusion between *V* the consonant and *V* the vowel.

W is the most recent of all letters of the alphabet. It was also the first (and only) letter to be used in Christopher Latham Sholes's first experimental prototype of his typewriter.

looking for **G** go to C

SPECIAL USES FOR **H**

H and **h** as abbreviations stand for: enthalpy, Hamiltonian, harbour, hard, hecto-, height, henry, heroin (slang), high, horn, hour, hundred, Hungary (international car registration), husband, hydrogen, magnetic field strength, Planck's constant

H is (usually) one of the few letters of the English alphabet whose name is not pronounced as the sound it makes.

PARTRIDGE'S
COMIC
ALPHABETS

H for retirement
(age for retirement)

The square angles of the letter H have their origins in *het*, an early pictograph that looked like this ⊞ and meant what it looked like — 'fence' or 'enclosure'.

The usual 90-degree turn occurred, and the 'fence' at first looked more like a ladder ⊟.

Later, the 'ladder' started to lose its four legs.

By the time the Greeks adopted it, the *H* looked like a domino ⊟. This soon lost the top and bottom cross-lines and became the letter *H,* which in Greek is a vowel called *eta*.

AH-HA, NOW IT ALL MAKES SENSE!

Remembering that the original letter was called *het*, it is not difficult to see the logic in both the Greeks making *eta* out of it, and the Romans making the consonant English speakers know as 'aitch' — however, in Latin, the 'h'-sound *was* pronounced in the name of the letter. The English way of saying 'aitch' stems from the French, who call the letter *hache*, and who do not pronounce the initial *h* on words starting with that letter. This, perhaps, gives ammunition to people who want to call it 'haitch', which is frowned upon by some: by pronouncing the *h,* not only is the original name of the letter restored, but also its sound in the English language.

looking for
J
go to I

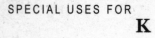

SPECIAL USES FOR **K**

K and **k** as abbreviations stand for: 1024 (computers), karat (US), Kelvin, kilo, kina, king, kip, Köchel, kopeck, kwatcha, kyat, Potassium

PARTRIDGE'S
COMIC
ALPHABETS

K for teria
(cafeteria)

K is not a komplikated karakter. It comes from a pictograph of the palm of a hand. The name was *kaf*, which means just that.

The picture was simplified until it looked like an imprint of a hand in the sand. After a while it lost some of its fingers so that it resembled a bird's foot.

In the usual fashion, the character was turned 90 degrees and started to look like an upside-down, mirror-reversed lower-case *k*.

The Greeks moved the 'fingers' to the centre of the character and called it *kappa*. When they later decided to write from left to right only, the modern *K* was a fact.

SPECIAL USES FOR
L

L and **l** as abbreviations stand for: 50 (Roman numerals), Avogadro's constant, lake, lambert, large, Latin, law, leaf, league, learner driver, left, lek, lempira, length, leu, liber, Liberal, licentiate, line, link, Linnaeus, lire, litre, live, lodge, low, Luxembourg (international car registration), pound (usually written £), self-inductance

PARTRIDGE'S
COMIC
ALPHABETS

L for leather
(hell for leather)

The letter *L* was derived from a hieroglyph depicting an ox-goad, that is, a stick with a handle at one end and a sharp point at the other. It was used to prod oxen into moving along to where they were supposed to go ⌒ .

There are dozens of variations of this character in historic documents, but they all have the long 'stick' with the curled 'handle' in common.

As was their wont, the Phoenicians turned the character around and simplified it. *L* was written by hook or ⌐⌐
by crook. ⌐ ⌐

When they first adopted the character, the Greeks used the *L* as it was, with the hook at the bottom. This was also the stage when the Etruscans imported the Greek alphabet.

Later, the Greeks turned the *L* upside down and lengthened the short leg to make a /\ *lambda*.

The Romans, however, imported the Etruscan version and

bɘƨɿɘvɘɿ-ɿoɿɿim

/\   /\   /

it to suit their left-to-right writing. Soon, the letter was stabilised to look like our modern *L*.

SPECIAL USES FOR Z

Z is called 'zed' in British and Australian English (from Old French *zede*), but 'zee' in American English. In the 15th century, **Z** was called *izzar* or *izzard* in England and France.

Z is often used repeatedly to signify sleep or the sound of snoring (as in 'Zzzzz' in comic strips, and 'pushing zeds', slang for sleeping)

Z and **z** as abbreviations stand for: anything unknown, atomic number, impedance, zaïre (currency), Zambia (international car registration), zero, zone

PARTRIDGE'S
COMIC
ALPHABETS

Z for the doctor
*(send for the doctor
[uttered with a
blocked nose])*

The letter Z might, according to some researchers, have something to do with an arrow, or an arrow going through a body. There is an Egyptian hieroglyph that means 'an arrow piercing skin' and looks like this.

Only the arrow remained after a while, and it was turned 90 degrees ⋏.

Then the angles of both the arrowhead and the feathers straightened out Ꞁ and lengthened ⊥.

The final step was that the vertical stroke became a diagonal, perhaps for the sake of expediency in handwriting (it could then be written in a single stroke), and the Z was a fact.

The Greeks called this character *zeta*. When the Romans acquired the Greek alphabet through the Etruscans, they had no use for the sound 'z', and discard-
ed the letter.
Only later,
when Latin
n e e d e d
some Greek
words (such
as 'zodiac'),
did the Ro-
mans rein-
state the let-
ter Z. They
stuck it at
the end of their alphabet, and that is why
Z is the seventh letter in the Greek alphabet
but the very last one in the Latin alphabet.

SPECIAL USES FOR **X**

X is a loose cannon when it comes to pronunciation. It can be pronounced as 'eks' ('x-ray'), as 'z' ('xylophone', 'xenophobe'), as 's' (the Greek letter *xi*), as 'h' or Scottish 'ch' (Spanish *Xeres* and *Ximenes* [now *Jerez* and *Jiménez*]), as 'k' ('Xhosa'), as 'sh' (Chinese words and place names), as 'ksh' ('inflexion', 'complexion'), and as 'cross' (X reference, X road)

X is probably the first choice when it comes to describing something unknown, as any Mister X knows. Wilhelm Konrad Röntgen called the strange light he had discovered 'X-rays' (in German, *X-Strahlen*), simply because he wasn't sure what these rays were.

X is also a common way of denoting 'kisses' in personal written communication (presumably because of its KisS sound).

Quite aside from something unknown, *X* is also used to signify a definite YES choice on forms and questionnaires.

However, *X* is a character with double meaning: while the student uses *X* to mean YES or CORRECT on the examination paper, the teacher uses it to mean NO or INCORRECT to mark a wrong answer.

X and **x** as abbreviations stand for:
10 (Roman numerals), adults only (as in X-rated), anything unknown, Christ, Christian, cross, error (as on an examination paper), kiss, selection or choice (as on a ballot paper or questionnaire).

The original symbol for *X* was, according to some researchers, a fishbone or maybe a ribcage. Whatever it was, it looked like this ⊤ .
When the Greeks ⊤ adopted the Phoenician alphabet, they made it first symmetrical and ⊥⊤ then lopped off the bits that were sticking out. ⊤ It became the Greek letter *xi*.

In western Greece the xi was written like an *X*.
The Romans initially had no use for an *X*. It was only imported in AD 100 to cope with Greek names such as Xenophon and Xanthippe.

SPECIAL USES FOR **C** and **G**

As abbreviations these letters stand for:

C and **c** — 100 (Roman numerals), capacitance, carat, carbon, caught, Celsius, cent, centi-, centigrade, century, chapter, circa, contralto, copyright (as in the © sign), coulomb, Cuba (international car registration), cubic, cycle

G and **g** — conductance, gallon, gauss, gelding, German, giga, good, government (as in G-man), gram, gravitational constant, guilder, guinea, gulf, thousand dollars or pounds (slang)

C

PARTRIDGE'S COMIC ALPHABETS

C for yourself
(see for yourself)
G for police
(chief of police)

Neck or hump? It's a hard choice.

Some historians claim that the letter *C* stands for camel, whatever part of the animal it depicts. ⚊⚊

In North Semitic, it looked like … well … just about anything with a bend in it ⌃.

The word for 'camel' in Hebrew and Arabic is *gamal*. The word for the letter *C* in Hebrew is *gimmel*. It is tempting to assume that the sign depicts either a camel's neck or hump.

The doubts start as soon as you realise that the camel was not a 'beast of burden' or a 'ship of the desert' until Roman times. There was no hieroglyph to depict the camel, although some sources say that perhaps the ancient Egyptians might have hunted wild camels for their meat.

Other researchers claim that the *C* is not a hump at all, but some sort of Egyptian weapon; a throwing-stick resembling a boomerang. This is a discussion that's sure to come back every now and then.

The Phoenician character was turned around, and by the time the Greeks got it, it had become what we know as the third Greek letter, *gamma* Γ.

In western Greece, however, the letter didn't quite make the full turn, and looked like a left angle-bracket on your keyboard ⟨. And this is the letter form that eventually became *C*.

But if this is the Greek letter *gamma*, and the Hebrew letter *gimmel*, we must be talking about the letter *G*, not *C*. What's the confusion?

The Etruscans are to blame. When the Etruscans, who lived in Italy, in what is now Tuscany, took over the Greek alphabet, they were at a loss what to do with *gamma*: the Etruscans had no 'g'-sound in their language. They decided to treat the letter as a voiceless 'g', that is, a 'k'-sound.

This meant that the Etruscans had three letters that all signified the 'k'-sound: *C*, *K* and *Q* (just as English has). They distinguished them as follows:

K was used in front of the letter *a*

C was used in front of the letters *e* and *i*

Q was used in front of the letter *u*

When the Romans imported the Etruscan alphabet to write their Latin language, things got a little complicated.

The trouble was that the Romans did have a 'g'-sound. But the Etruscans had made the original Greek *gamma* into a *C*.

For a while, the Romans used the alphabet in the Etruscan way. For instance, they spelt the name Caius with a *C*, although it was pronounced 'Gaius'. After some time, the Romans got a bit confused themselves, and placed a little cross-bar on the *C* to make a *G*, if it was pronounced that way.

They now had a brand new letter in their alphabet.

Where to put the new *G*? The Romans realised that they had one Greek letter that they did not use in Latin: *zeta*, which was the seventh letter of the alphabet. They got rid of *zeta* and replaced it with *G*.

Later, the Romans began to import Greek loanwords into Latin and found that they needed *zeta* after all. They re-incorporated the letter, but because its original place was now occupied by *G*, they attached *zeta* at the end of the alphabet — and that is why the English alphabet runs from *A* to *Z*, but the Greek alphabet does not.

LOWER-CASE g

The lower-case *g* looks very different from upper-case G. There are two major kinds of lower-case: a style often called 'single-storey' such as Ɋ, and a beautiful, curly 'double-storey'. g

It is the latter that best shows the origin of the lower-case *g*.

The Romans had no lower-case. They used only capital G — the C with an extra cross-bar, as explained above.

They did, however, have two different ways of forming the letter, depending on the writing materials used: with a hammer and chisel and a slab of stone, they wrote G. With a pen or a brush and a piece of papyrus, they wrote Ϛ.

The horizontal line at the top of this version is reminiscent of the horizontal cross-bar of the G used for chiselling monuments. It is this line that can be seen in the 'double-storey' *g*. The Carolingian minuscule (lower-case) script *g* of the 8th century was ᒼ.

From there, the step was not far to either of our modern main types of the letter

B

looking for
V
go to F

SPECIAL USES FOR B

B is often used to signify inferiority or second choice (B-grade movie, B-side of a record, B-road).

B and **b** as abbreviations stand for: bass, bay, Belgium (international car registration), Bible, billion, bishop, black, bomber (as in B-52), born, boron, bowled, British, bye

PARTRIDGE'S
COMIC
ALPHABETS

B for mutton
(beef or mutton)

The letter *B* stems from a hieroglyph depicting a house. It was an architect's floor-plan of a simple and unpretentious one-room place: an Egyptian bachelor flat, if you like. There is an entrance, a little hallway where you hang your coat and keep your goat, and a single bedroom inside ⌐⊔.

Although the Egyptians had pronounced this character as a deep 'h' sound (as in 'hot'), the North Semitic word for 'house' was *bayit*, which corresponds to Hebrew *beth* (as in Bethlehem) and Arabic *bait*. Later, the word for the letter became the Greek *beta*.

Over time the hieroglyph was simplified and made more aesthetically pleasing by balancing the proportions. It also became easier to write ▱.

As became a common phenomenon, the letter was turned this way and that, and even mirror-reversed.

By the time the North Semites were finished with it, *B* looked like this ⟨ .

When the Greeks adopted the letter, it turned again, and the top began to curl.
In fact, it curled so much
that it closed up altogether.

A little later, when the Greeks finally decided to write from left to right, they reversed the letter, and it became our familiar *B*.

B

SPECIAL USES FOR N

N and **n** as abbreviations stand for: Avogadro's number, indefinite number (as in 'there are n objects in the box'), knight, nano-, nationalist, *natus*, navy, neper, neuter, neutral, neutron, new, newton, nitrogen, nominative, noon, Norse, north, Norway (international car registration), note, noun, number

PARTRIDGE'S
COMIC
ALPHABETS

N for mation
(information)

The original hieroglyph was that of a cobra.

In Egyptian it was pronounced like the English 'j'.
In North Semitic it was called *nun*.

When the hieroglyph was alphabetised, it underwent a simplification process. The soft, rounded curves
of the snake became more acute ㄥㄥ.

The letter was written in several directions. As with
M and *K,* the Phoenicians liked to lengthen one of
the legs ㄣ

When the Greeks took on the character, they
shortened the long leg and made the letter
symmetrical.

As with so many other letters, some time after the
Greeks decided to write left-to-right only, the *N* was
stabilised into the form we know today.

M

m

SPECIAL USES FOR M

M and **m** as abbreviations stand for: 1000 (Roman numerals), maiden, majesty, male, Malta (international car registration), Manitoba, mare, mark, marquis, married, masculine, master, mature, medieval, medicine, medium, mega-, member, meridian, metre, middle, mile, million, molar, Monday, Monsieur, month, motorway, mutual inductance

PARTRIDGE'S
COMIC
ALPHABETS

M for sis
(emphasis)

The letter *M* derives from an Egyptian hieroglyph that looks very much like *M*. In fact, it looks like several *M*s in a row ᨈᨆᨆ .

The hieroglyph, not surprisingly, meant 'water' or 'waves' but was pronounced 'n'.

This was a favourite hieroglyph; one of the most common. In fact, it was so popular that it was often doubled and even tripled ∿∿∿ to mean anything to do with water, ∿∿∿ or liquids, or actions relating to liquids. ∿∿∿ The character was used to describe thirst or the water level of the Nile, or drink or quench, or extinguish fire, or harvest.

The *M* is one of the few characters that survived the 90-degree turn. It was indeed put on its end at first, but then landed back on its feet again.

As with *K* and *N*, the Phoenicians liked to have one 'leg' of the character longer than the other.

When the Greeks adopted *M*, they snipped off the long leg to make the character

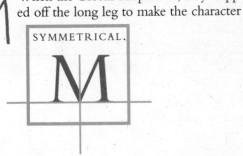

SYMMETRICAL.

However, the original long leg lives on in the Greek lower-case *mu* μ.

Punctuation ma

! to €

rks and symbols

on the

[O] [A] [R] [D]

and

beyond

!

The exclamation mark used to
be known as a 'bang' or a
'screamer' among printers.

For some special uses of !, and for
information on the ¡Spanish!
upside-down exclamation mark
and the interrobang, see the
section on the question mark.

An exclamation mark is used
to indicate factorials in maths
equations, as in 2!.

What's the answer?
That's the question!

The exclamation mark is much younger than its cousin, the question mark. Sure is! It dates from the second half of the 14th century.

The exclamation mark might be the only punctuation mark that can be attributed to one single originator. If copyright had been around in the late 1300s, the exclamation mark might have been written

! © 1380 by Iacopo Alpoleio da Urbisaglia

Iacopo wrote about the need for a sign that could express a strong and positive statement. He must have felt very endeared to his new mark, because he named it *punctus admirativus* and declared that it should comprise two strong dots at the bottom and a swish virgule at the top.

Graphic designers and typographic historians sometimes say that the *punctus exclamativus*, as it was also known, was actually an *I* on top of an *o*, thus representing the Latin word *io*, which means 'hooray!' or 'joy!'.

I
o

However attractive and feasible this theory might appear, old manuscripts do not seem to support it.

SPECIAL USES FOR @

Used to denote 'in exchange for',
as in 'orange juice @ $1 per litre'.

Used in email addresses to
separate an individual mailbox
from the domain to which it
belongs, or a 'name' from a
'home', as in *fido@itsadogslife.com*

In Laos an *at* is a hundredth of a
kip.

At is the chemical symbol for
astatine.

The c@ s@ on the m@.
& th@'s where it's @!

PET NAMES

The @ symbol has many names around the world.
Here are a few examples.

Bulgarian	*majmunka* (little monkey)
Catalan	*ensaïmada* (sort of filled pastry of the Balearic Islands)
Chinese	*huā A* (flower-*A*)
	A quān (circle-*A*)
Czech	*zavináč* (rollmops — from *zavin*, strudel)
Dutch	*apestaartje* (monkey's tail)
English	*at*
	commercial at
	strudel
	cinnamon bun
Finnish	*miuku-mauku* (meow)
French	*arobase* (old weight measure; see Spanish)
	A commercial
	escargot (snail)
German	*Klammeraffe* (spider monkey)
	Affenschwantz (monkey's tail)
Inuit	*A-jusaq* (*A*-like*)*
Italian	*chiocciola* (snail)
Korean	*dal phaeng i* (snail)
Norwegian	*alfa krøll* (alpha curl)
	grisehale (pig's tail)
Portuguese	*arroba* (see Spanish)
Russian	*lyagushka* (frog)
	soba[ch]ka ([little] dog)
	ushko (little ear)
	obez'yana (monkey)
Spanish	*arroba* (old weight measure; from Arabic: a quarter [of a quintal])
Swedish	*snabela* (elephant's trunk *a*)
Turkish	*at* (horse)
	kulak (ear)

As an erstwhile little-used symbol on the keyboard,
the @ has enjoyed a spectacular resurrection — so much
so that when Olympic fever hit the United States in
1996, '@lanta' was the place to be in many American eyes
(does that mean it will be @hens in 2004?).

The reason is, of course, the emergence of @ as the ubiquitous character in every email address in the whole wide world.

Perhaps this character started its life as the letter-line combination that was very common in word contractions $\overline{a}$.

Typographic historians differ in their opinions about the origin of this little character. Some say that it is short for the Latin word *ad*, which means 'at' or 'towards', and that the curl is the upstroke of the *d* embracing the *a*.

Others claim that the sign is short for *ana*, which means 'in equal quantity' in medieval Latin, derived from the Greek meaning 'of every one similarly', and is still used in medicine and pharmaceutics, often expressed through the abbreviation $\overline{aa}$.

Each theory has its merit, both in terms of trail of pen and train of thought. Take your pick.

SAVED @ THE LAST MINUTE

The @ symbol first made its debut on the keyboard in the late 1800s. However, it never really caught on and its use dwindled. The sign might have disappeared altogether from the keyboard if it wasn't for a young computer pioneer in 1971. Ray Tomlinson, involved in developing the concept of email at the computer firm Bolt, Beranek & Newman, pondered over his keyboard, trying to think up a convenient way of addressing emails, so that they could be sent first to the correct server, and then to the relevant addressee. How to keep the name separate from the address? It wasn't long before the @ leapt from almost complete obscurity to one of the most 'with-it' symbols in modern history.

Tomlinson sent messages to himself from one wardrobe-size computer in the room to another. His first email was addressed to tomlinson@bbn-tenexa.

SPECIAL USES FOR #

Used to signify 'number'
— as in #24.

Used by proofreaders to add
space between lines or letters.

Note: the # is not the same as the
musical sharp ♯.

In mathematics the # signifies
equal and parallel.

In HTML the # is used:
• to signify 'jump to bookmark'
  on the current web page, for
  example, # next heading

• together with the & to signify
  character codes, for example,
  &# 229; (to write å).

The strokes and
dashes number four
In writing hashes:
'#4'

There are several names for this symbol:

> hash
>
> pound sign
>
> number/numeral sign
>
> space sign
>
> octothorp

The name 'hash' comes from hatch, as in cross-hatching; the name 'pound' comes from Latin; the term 'octothorp' is a Latin–Scandinavian hybrid; and explanation for the other names leave themselves open to speculation.

THEORY #1 — THE POUND

The old Italian weight measure was the *libbra*, roughly corresponding to today's pound weight. Italian shipping clerks abbreviated the word to *lb* (the same as the symbol 'lb' used in the United Kingdom and the United States for 'pound') and drew a horizontal line across the two letters to indicate the contraction *℔*. Swiftly written, the symbol took on its present shape *℔* ⇒ *#*.

Note that the British pound symbol *£* is related to the # sign. It stems from the Latin *lībra pondō* (a pound in weight). Keyboards in the United Kingdom have this symbol in place of the # key on American, Australian and many other keyboards.

THEORY #2 — THE OCTOTHORP

Some people believe that the # sign depicts eight homesteads around a village common

Hence the *octothorp*; *octo* from the Latin word for eight, and *thorp* from the Norse word for homestead or croft. The village square in the centre is empty, which could account for the sign sometimes meaning 'space'.

The $ is not only used for
'dollar'; it is also used in many
other places, particularly where
the peso is the national currency
(for obvious reasons — see below).

In computing the $ is used to
signify a reserved or otherwise
special value, as in $firstname.

Dollar signs are
very nice
In your purse
(not in your eyes)

The dollar sign has an interesting history that begins in 1519 in Bohemia.

In the little town of St Joachimsthal a large silver coin was minted for the first time. This silver coin was intriguingly called a *Gulden*, but soon came to be known as a *Joachimsthaler* to mark its birthplace.

The longish name was later shortened to *Joachsthaler*, and then simply *thaler*.

When Denmark and Sweden started to mint their own coinages, they adopted the name and called their money *daler*. The Dutch called it *daalder*. This is where the word 'dollar' comes from.

The dollar sign, with its characteristic *S* and two vertical lines, has nothing to do with the Joachimsthaler, nor is it an *S*.

When the Spaniards started to mint their own coins, they did so in the West Indies. The first Spanish coins were called *Peso de Plata*, which simply describes what the coins were: a piece of silver. (The Spanish currency, the peseta, means 'little piece'.)

From the West Indies, the step was not far to America in the north. The coin came to be called a 'piece of eight', because there were eight reals to one peso.

A piece of eight could be written P8 for short, and soon there was a symbol that was a combination of a *P* and an 8.

This seemed rather difficult to write, however, and the Americans started writing their piece of eight in a more convenient way /8/.

A hastily written 8 can easily become an *S*-like swirl, and this is just what happened. At the same time, writers started to move the two slanted strokes around, and soon the dollar sign took on its final, familiar shape.

Some people believe that the dollar sign stems from a combination of *U* and *S*, as in the United States, but this supposition seems to have no support in typographical history documents.

The double vertical lines of the dollar sign are disappearing. They are becoming rare in modern typefaces for practical reasons: printing is a mechanical process, and ink is a liquid. The fine features of the dollar sign are likely to fill in between the lines when printed in a small size, and a single stroke is much easier to print while still making an unmistakable dollar sign.

Many typefaces have even got rid of the middle (or muddle) part of the stroke.

The per cent sign comes from the Italian *numero per cento*, which means 'this number in a hundred'.

The word *numero* was often contracted to its first and last letters, and we still use the symbol for the word 'number'.

N⁰

In the beginning *numero per cento* was written thus.

N%

Later its *N* was dropped on its way to becoming the per cent sign on our keyboard today.

%

%

In a poll,
per cent is nifty
(just make sure
you're over fifty)

116

SPECIAL USES FOR &

In mathematics the & is used to signify a conjunction of statements.

In HTML the & is used together with the # to signify character codes, for example, #&246; (to write ö).

In computer programming the & is used in query strings to separate sets of keys and values; for example, in a search procedure: city=moscow&country=russia.

The Ampersand Mountains can be found in Franklin County, New York State, USA.

The difference
soon you'll
understand,
'tween ' '
and 'and',
and 'and' and '&'

The word 'ampersand' is a peculiar mixture of Latin & English. The central part of the word comes from Latin *per se* which means 'in itself'. Stick an 'and' at either end, and you get 'and per se and', which doesn't mean much at first glance.

Perhaps it becomes clearer if we write:

& in itself [stands for] 'and'

Say 'and per se and' quickly, and you get ampersand.

The curly symbol (in itself) is derived from an *E* and a *T*, making up the Latin word *et*, which means — surprise, surprise — 'and'.

In early ampersands the *E* and the *T* are clearly discernible, as they are in some of the modern typefaces we use today.

AMPERSNOT

The character ⅋ so often used in longhand is not a simplified version of an ampersand, but a sign that was used by English scribes.

At first, the word 'and' was abbreviated to Ⱦ. The lines soon merged and became a sort of plus sign. When written quickly without taking the pen off the paper, this took on the familiar 'and' shape.

Now
your
eyes
will
travel
far*

SPECIAL USES FOR *

The * is one of a suite of symbols, including the †, used instead of numbers to indicate footnotes in the text.

Commonly used as a 'wildcard' in computer commands (as in *aster**, which gives *aster, asteria, asterisk, asterism, astern, asteroid,* and so on).

Also used in statistics to mark level of probability.

* Looking for a little star

The word 'asterisk' means what the symbol looks like: a little star (or stars**) in the text. It has been used for centuries to signify some sort of omission. In his *Etymologiae*, St Isidore of Seville (*ca* 560–636) described the role of the asterisk beautifully: 'The asterisk is placed against [that which has been] omitted in order for what seems to be omitted may shine forth.'

Another use for the asterisk is to mark that a certain individual letter has been left out of a word, as in f***-letter words.

It is St Isidore's 'shining forth' that is important: the asterisk usually signifies something that seems to have been left out, but is sure to become evident in one form or another: as the results of a 'wildcard' search; as a footnote; as a four-letter word in your mind.

DO YOU BELIEVE IN ASTERISM?

A constellation of three asterisks can be put to use in an 'asterism' *** which is a rare sign marking some thing of particular interest in the text that follows.

Also a good conversation point at a party that lacks sparkle.

HAVE A BREAK, HAVE A DINKUS

Three (or more) asterisks in a row are often used to break up the text in books.

* * *

When used in this way, the group of asterisks (and sometimes other symbols, swirls, twirls, flourishes, curlicues or little drawings) is called a 'dinkus' or 'dingus'.

** the word comes from Greek *asteriskos*, diminutive of *aster* 'star'. Before it became the familiar little star, the asterisk had another look ✳ or ✲

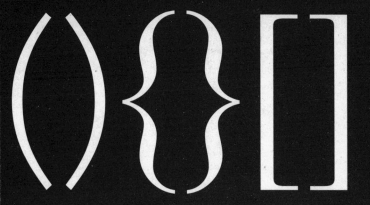

SPECIAL USES FOR (){}[]

a) The use of the parenthesis (or parentheses) is well-known.

Square brackets [often] mark editorial additions or interpolations, for example, to point out misstakes [*sic*] in the original text.

Curly brackets are sometimes used to link { two three many } items as options on separate lines.

Always keep your
private fantasies
Hidden well
(within parentheses)

All of these coupled signs can be described as brackets:

( ) parentheses or round brackets

[ ] square brackets or crotchets

{ } braces or curly brackets

When these brackets are used together to enclose text or for aggregations in mathematics, it is normally in the following order: {[()]}.

The word *parenthesis* means 'a putting in beside' in Greek.

The parenthesis (used in singular to mean a pair of left-and-right parentheses) appeared around 1500. While most of the basic signs were originally designed as aids to inflexion and intonation (that is, guides to show how to read a text aloud), the parentheses were the product of the growing practice of silent reading.

At first, either / or : was used as parentheses, but this was confusing, because those signs also served as the comma and the full stop, respectively.

New marks had to be devised. The earliest ones had a different left and right bracket ⌐ they looked like this ⌐.

The two were later paired up to ⟨ ⟩ and in time became rounded (they were known as *virgula convexae*).

Known as 'underline', 'low line',
or 'underscore'

Used on typescripts as a
proofreader's mark to indicate
italics.

A double underline indicates small
capitals. A triple underline indicates capitals.

Used as a space character in
email_addresses and long_
file_names.

Used on either side of a word to
signify _emphasis_ in emails, if
bold or italics cannot be used.

I know a most
important sign:
It's called
the dreaded
bottom line.

How could you possibly use the <u>underscore</u> character on a computer keyboard? You certainly can't use it to underline a word or a phrase for <u>emphasis</u>.

Underlining important and noteworthy text comes naturally: it can be seen as clearly in ancient manuscripts as it is in today's newspaper.

And it is simple enough to produce an underscore with a pen, or to use the backspace on a typewriter and do a few _____ underneath the already typed text.

Not so on the computer. The underline is a character without a job: an underline without anything to underline.

It may seem strange, then, that the underscore has remained on the keyboard. But like the @ sign and the ~ tilde, the underscore has found alternative employment: it is commonly used as a space character in computer filenames_where_spaces are not permitted, and sometimes preceding _hidden folders or directories.

The word 'hyphen' comes from the Greek. It means 'together', and is made up of *hypo-* ('under') and *hen* ('one').

Used to signify 'minus' in mathematics, when no minus sign is available on the keyboard.

If lines are long, just use a hyphen as you would a cutting knife.

In Latin manuscripts there was no call for hyphens. There were no word-spaces, and the text could be broken anywhere

```
THE TEXT JUSTRA
NONANDONWI THO
UTANYREGARDFO
RWHEREWORDSBE
GANANDENDEDOR
FORUGLYBREAKS
```

It wasn't until late in the 10th century, when the word-space had been invented, that scribes began to use a little mark to denote that a word had to be broken at the end of one line and continued at the start of the next. Later, from the 14th to the 18th century, two lines (= or ⁄) were often used for this purpose.

The plus and the minus signs were, like the 'ditto' sign, invented by Italian shipping clerks.

When a load of cargo was a little over the stipulated weight, the clerks wrote P̄ for 'plus' (or *più*, which means 'more' in Italian). The 'abbreviation line' dropped, and the curve of the *P* shrank, leaving a plus sign. P̄ ⇒ ┣ ⇒ ╋ . If the load was short on weight, the clerks wrote M̄ for 'minus' (or *meno* in Italian, meaning 'less'). After a while, the upper-case *M* was written in lower-case, then dropped altogether, leaving a nice companion to the plus sign. ᴧᴧ ⇒ — Of course, if you are the indecisive type, the ± sign might be more or less appropriate.

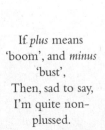

If *plus* means
'boom', and *minus*
'bust',
Then, sad to say,
I'm quite non-
plussed.

127

The equals sign (also called equal sign) was first introduced in the 16th century by the English mathematician Robert Recorde in his work of 1557, entitled *The Whetstone of Witte*. In this book Recorde writes 'I will sette as I doe often in woorke use, a paire of paralleles, or Gemowe [old word for 'twin'] lines of one lengthe, thus: ――――――――――― , bicause noe. 2. thynges, can be moare equalle.'

The two parallel lines were made as long as the available space, perhaps to distinguish the equal sign from the popular 'double hyphen', although this was often written with a slant ⌿.

Maths professors
get fed up
If their equals
don't add up

The | is known as vertical bar,
vertical line, and other names.

The ¦ is known as vertical bar,
broken bar, parted rule, and other
names.

The \ is known as backslash
(as one word or two), back stroke,
back slant, reverse solidus, and
other names.

Here we are
at the Vertical Bar,
So what shall we
have to drink?
Just a dash
Of backward slash,
In a vertical jar,
I think.

These two characters (if you accept that the broken bar is a variant of the vertical line) occur as a special key on many keyboards. Both characters have to do with computer programming.

A BACKWARD BENT

The backslash character did not appear on any computer until 1958, when it entered the character set of the IBM Stretch 7030 computer. The man who put it there was programmer Robert W. Bemer, who refers to the backslash as 'my character' in his *Computer History Vignettes*. It was originally used in combination with the forward slash to make the two logical symbols /\ and \/ in the ALGOL computer programming language. /\ meant AND, and \/ meant OR.

As computers developed, there was no longer a need for using two characters to write a command symbol, and the backslash might have fallen into desuetude. But the opposite happened: with the emergence of Microsoft's MS-DOS system, the 'obsolete' backslash was the perfect candidate for a most important job: to specify subdirectories in path names, such as C:\DOS\utilities\fdisk.exe.

LINE UP!

There is confusion about the vertical line and the vertical broken bar: on many keyboards, the key itself shows a broken bar ¦ but prints a vertical line | when you press it. On older computers, the character appeared as a ¦ on the screen as well. The two variants, however, are separate characters in the ASCII character set.

In DOS and UNIX commands, the vertical bar is used for 'piping'. For instance, the command

```
type quirky.txt ¦ more
```

means that the computer will 'pipe' the text file *quirky.txt* to the more function, which will place as much text as will fit on the computer screen and then stop, waiting for you to press a key for the next screen-ful of text.

The sign is also used to signify logical choices, such as **item1** | **item2** | **item3**. This fashion is very familiar to internet users. On millions of web pages, the vertical bar is used to separate various choices of hyperlinks.

<u>Home</u> | <u>Products</u> | <u>Services</u> | <u>Contacts</u>

In addition, the character has uses outside computing as well. In dictionaries, for instance, it may be used to signify the division between the root or invariable part of a word and its possible endings or suffixes: *typ | e –ing –ist*.

SPECIAL USES FOR :

Used to separate the main title of a book or film from the subtitle, as in *Mind the Stop: a brief guide to punctuation.*

Used in time expressions, as in *11:30 am* (chiefly in America)

Used to indicate Bible verses — *Ruth 2:12*

Used to express ratio, as in *The aspect ratio of a TV screen is 3:4* and *The scale of this map is 1:500.*

The word 'colon' stems from the Greek *kōlon*, which means 'clause'. Modern Greek has no colon.

There's no doubt,
no ifs or buts:
The colon's got a
lot of guts.

Aristophanes of Byzantium, the librarian at the library of Alexandria around 200 BC, first used the word *kōlon*, to describe one of his three marks that distinguished sections of three different lengths in rhetorical theory: *komma* (a dot at mid-height in the text) marked the short section; *kōlon* (a dot at the baseline) marked the longer section, and *periodos* (at the top) marked the end of the longest section. The colon used by Aristophanes was, therefore, not really a punctuation mark, although our colon is named after it.

The shape of our colon has its origin in a punctuation mark called *punctus elevatus* and looked something like this ∴ .

Confusingly, old manuscripts also contain a punctuation mark : which looks exactly like our colon, but was the full stop of the time. The text following it started with an upper-case letter.

Adding to the punctuation frenzy in the 1200s, the colon also served as a parenthesis, before the parentheses were invented.

The ; is the Greek way of writing a question mark. The ? is not used in Greek.

The Greek semicolon is a high point · (the colon is not used in Greek).

The semicolon was a compromise; it served as a convenient mean between two extremes. At the end of the 15th century, the virgule (/) was used to signify a comma, and the two colon-like dots (:) were the full stop. There was nothing in between, and the ; was a suitable medium (the term 'semicolon' means, of course, half-colon or, in effect, half a full stop). It became a very popular sign; today, however, many writers never use the semicolon at all.

Semicolon; it
makes you laugh
A kind of colon,
but only half

SPECIAL USES " " ' < > « » ‹ ›

< and **>** are often used to signify a key on the keyboard, as in 'Press <ENTER>'.

" is used in tables and lists to duplicate the data given above (see over page).

' is used to indicate a minute of an arc (in mathematics, as in 35° 10') or in time; and to indicate a foot in old imperial measurements (5' high).

" is used to indicate a second of an arc (in mathematics, as in 35° 10' 2"), or in time; and to indicate an inch in old imperial measurements (5' 10" high).

Single quotes and
double
Cause a lot of
trouble
Words (you might
not mean them)
May end up
between them

The quotation marks started out around 100 BC as something called a 'diple'.

A diple? You won't find the word in any concise dictionary. It is a term used by palaeographers to describe a mark that looked a bit like a right chevron (>). Sometimes it had a dot or a line between its legs and sometimes it was more rounded, like a horse shoe, and had a line in the centre.

The lower leg was often drawn with a flourish.

The diple was used in French well into the 1800s, although in England it started to fall out of favour in the early 18th century.

This mark was used to point out something especially 'noteworthy' in the text — perhaps to indicate what someone had said. It usually appeared in the margin, and usually marked only the beginning of an important statement. In other words, there was no pair of diples that opened and closed the statement.

Over time, the > got a sibling in < and these were soon doubled up: they became *«guillemets»*, which are still used in modern French and other languages to mark quotations.

The single and double quotation marks used in English can be seen as rounded versions of the *guillemets*. The 'convex' arrangement opening and closing a statement is the same.

CONFUSION

The quotation marks went through some teething problems. Scribes weren't too sure how to use them. Initially, the quotation mark was used along with the diple. Then the mark was used to replace the diple altogether, but was still written in the margin.

The marks that we now call 'opening and closing quotation marks' were sometimes used at every line, depending on whether they appeared on a left-hand page (or column) or a right-hand one.

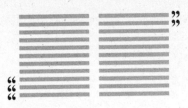

SINGLES VS DOUBLES

Why do we have single and double quotes? In the mid-1700s, there was a big difference: 'single' quotes were used for reported speech, and "double" quotes for direct speech.

The distinction (although singles and doubles can be freely interchanged) is still seen in modern English:

> "I will sue you for calling me a 'silly old bugger' even if it ruins me," the senior citizen said to the prime minister.

or

> 'I will sue you for calling me a "silly old bugger" even if it ruins me,' the senior citizen said to the prime minister.

WATCH YOUR DIPLES!

It is important to remember that quotes are done differently in different languages. The English quotation marks or inverted commas are often not appropriate in other tongues.

FRENCH uses «guillemets» or — dashes to mark direct speech (a practice also used by James Joyce, who disliked quotation marks: he called them 'perverted commas').

GERMAN is a bit tricky: it also uses »guillemets« but turned inside out, or low and high pairs of „commas" where the first pair is **not** inverted.

SWEDISH also uses quotation marks as in English, but watch it!. The first pair of "commas" is not inverted.

Swedish also makes use of the — dash to indicate direct speech in dialogue.

RUSSIAN and many other Slavonic languages, whether using Cyrillic or Latin script, accept all of the above, except the German inverted guillemets and the English inverted commas.

WHY IS " USED IN TABLES?

In a table or list, a pair of closing quotes " is used to repeat the data given directly above. The origin of this shortcut has nothing to do with quotation marks, but is the invention of Italian clerks who started off writing the word *ditto*, which means 'aforesaid', in the columns of their ledgers instead of duplicating the numbers or words in the cell above.

But even writing *ditto* a hundred times every day was hard work, so the clerks abbreviated the word by taking the first and last letters, making *do* with that.

Writing countless lists, the Italian clerks found that even two letters were too long, and *do* for *ditto* soon became "

ᵈo ᵈo ᵈ•)ı "

SPECIAL USES ,

Commonly used to show where letters, or parts of words, or figures have been omitted, as in it's (for it is), or 'phone (for telephone) or '64 (for 1964).

Used in many languages to signify a glottal stop.

Used to signify the soft sign in transliteration of Cyrillic writing, as in Russian *mat'* ('mother') as opposed to *mat* (abusive expression).

There's an English word with THREE apostrophes: fo'c's'le (short for 'forecastle', the sailors' quarters in a ship's prow).

Tahiti's airport's name's Fa'a'a.

Apostrophe abuse:
Its best to know
it's use

The apostrophe was the Greeks' invention. They used their word for 'elide' for this little sign that signifies omission (or elision) of one or more letters.

Its use is often a writer's licence to skip a bit ('o'er the rainbow', 'he shopp'd 'til he dropp'd', 'playin' the rock'n'roll').

When used to mark possession, the apostrophe replaces a whole word. When we write 'Murphy's law', we mean 'Murphy *his* law'.

APOSTROFLATION

In her book *Australian English Style Guide* Pam Peters calls it apostroflation: the ever-spreading use

BBQ CHICKEN'S
FISH'n'CHIP'S
Lots'n'lotsa'postrophe's

(and abuse) of apostrophes where they don't belong.

,

SPECIAL USES FOR

,

Used in many languages to separate
groups of digits in large numbers,
as in 120,594,732.

Often used as a separator in
databases, for instance — table 22,
pizza, large, mexicana.

The word 'comma' comes from
Greek *komma* ('clause')

A comma is a ratio by which an
instrument is mistuned. Even a
mistuning by 80:81 can be very
disagreeable to a human (Western)
ear.

Commas can be
really cool
Cut it out and call
me, fool!

The comma is our 'lightest' punctuation mark. Through history, there have been many different kinds of comma. Irish monks in the Dark Ages used a tiny mark with a heavy name: *simplex ductus* looked like a little seven 7 inserted where a brief pause was appropriate. This was to become a common comma. It became so common that it was often used twice 77 or even three times 777 to signify a slightly longer pause (because the 'sevens' were written without lifting the pen, they came to look almost like our cursive *n* and *m*).

Between AD 1000 and 1200, two new marks, *punctus flexus* (⌒) and *punctus elevatus* (.⌣) were used for brief pauses, depending on the sentence structure and the required inflexion.

The use of a single virgule (/) to serve the role of the comma was very popular in the 15th century and into the 16th century.

Our modern comma comes from a variant of the virgule, used by Italian scribes in the 14th century. They used a curved virgule above a dot (⸒). Over time, the curve started to sink downwards towards the baseline of the text, thus forming our familiar comma.

NEW-COMMAS WELCOME

The invention of the printing press meant that punctuation needed to be cleaned up and the chaotic jumble of little handwritten marks was slowly sifted down to just a few basic, printed ones.

All of the signs that had previously served as guides for reading the text aloud (where to breathe, how long to pause, what pitch of the voice to use, and so on) had become obsolete with the coming of silent reading; the role of punctuation marks had changed from inflexional (how to say it) to syntactical (how to understand it).

However, simplification did not suit everyone. The Frenchman J. H. Chauvier found in the first half of the 19th century what he called a 'serious inconvenience' in the punctuation system, and wrote a book about it. In his work *A Treatise on Punctuation: in which is Explained Clearly what is a Sentence, or its Member, a Period, or its Member; what Signs must Follow these Elements of Discourse; and the Only Law which Governs the Use of the Signs.*, Monsieur Chauvier (doubtless a great aficionado of long and amply punctuated book titles) praises the benefits of a punctuation standard, but laments the lack of a reversed comma.

A reversed comma? Chauvier argued that just as there was a pair of left and right parentheses, there ought to be a pair of commas as well: a standard comma and its counterpart, curved the other way — a *reversed* one.

The reversed comma, claimed Chauvier, would make it easy to spot *incidentals*, as he called it, and his book is full of the peculiar pairs of commas. This is how they worked —

Silence ˏneedless to say, is golden.

As we know, Monsieur Chauvier's comma-caper was *un flop*. There is sadly, no reversed comma even on the most sophisticated keyboard.

FULL

STOP

SPECIAL USES FOR

•

- in numbered lists such as 1. and
  A. and 1.5.8 and 4.d.
- time and date, such as 5.30 p.m.
  and 22.11.2001
- dollars and cents: $33.40
- decimal point: 0.56
- to signify an abbreviated word
  (but not a contraction).

How the full stop should be used
in abbreviations is a discussion that
will never come to a .

The . is never used in:
- SI units (kg, ml, km, etc.)
- compass points
- acronyms (such as laser and
  nimby – not l.a.s.e.r. and
  n.i.m.b.y.)

Just a little dot
Stops you.
On the spot.

144

It's small. It's powerful. It stops you in your tracks.

At least, that's what the full stop (or full point, or period) ought to do, according to the broadcaster Art Linkletter, who said:

> *A period is to let a writer know he has finished his thought and he should stop there if he will only take the hint.*

The full stop has appeared in many guises over the centuries.

Irish monks in the Dark Ages used a combination of several dots, such as .., or :, as a kind of a full stop. Later, the *punctus versus* 7 or ⁊ was the major stop.

After AD 1200 the full stop was often written as two virgules // and some Italian reformists preferred to use a horizontal virgule at the end of sentences —

The twin slanted lines // were quite popular. They later changed into two dots that looked like a colon : and were used extensively.

Our single dot was the result of Manutius's orthography system in the late 1500s.

DOT DOT DOT

Three full stops in a row form an 'ellipsis', which is a way of showing that something in a text has been deliberately omitted.

> 'Your essay should be … short, sharp and succinct,' said the teacher.

(In the example above, the ellipsis might get rid of 'anything but longwinded, verbose, prolix, overblown, wordy, rambling and tedious. Instead it should be'.)

The ellipsis can be seen as a companion to the asterisk. While the asterisk is used to signify omission of something that can be found elsewhere (as in the footnote) or gathered intuitively (as in a f***-letter word), the ellipsis shows that something has been left out to stay out, full stop.

SPECIAL USES FOR ?

In chess notation, ? and ! are very efficiently used. For example, 'rook takes pawn':

R x P! (good move) R x P!! (excellent move) R x P?! (iffy move, but might work) R x P!? (unusual move; seems good, but risky) R x P? (a mistake) R x P?? (no question: a complete foot-shootin' blunder)

In 1862 the French novelist Victor Hugo was anxious to find out how his new novel *Les Misérables* was selling. He decided to write a letter to his publishers Hurst & Blackett. He wrote '?'.
The reply was '!'.

Give the answer,
prompt and early,
Why the question
is so curly?

The question mark dates back to a sign introduced in the 1200s called *punctus interrogativus*. It may have been designed to illustrate the rise in inflexion at the end of a question: ✔ or ∿ .

After the invention of the movable-type printing press, the question mark slowly took on its modern shape.

Many typographers and typographic historians believe that the question mark stems from the Latin word *quaestio* ('question') and was abbreviated by writing the first letter of the word above the last ꝗ .

This is a tantalising proposition: the *q* really does look a bit like the curl of the ?, and the *o* could easily be the dot. Old manuscripts, however, provide no support for this theory.

The medieval question mark had an additional function that has since been lost: a mirror-reversed question mark (called *punctus percontativus*) signified a rhetorical question that did not expect a direct answer.

Am I my brother's keeper ⸮

Such a creative use of the question mark is now absent from our writing system. However, we do have the 'interrobang' ‽ .

The interrobang was a new punctuation mark proposed by printers and typographers in the 1960s. The name never caught on, nor did the typographical design. However, the **use** of a question mark and exclamation mark together is quite common:

You want it when?!

¿WHAT ABOUT THE SPANISH QUESTION?
The upside-down Spanish question mark was introduced in 1754. Prior to this, a single question mark at the end of the sentence had been used — but the method did not quite suit the Spanish language, and for a good reason.

In order to correctly understand and pronounce a question, a Spanish reader has to know from the outset whether the phrase is a question or a statement. This can be difficult, even if the sentence begins with a question word.

What could be done was to design an initial punctuation mark that would signal a question.

¿What could be done to find such a device that would, at the beginning of a sentence, signal a question?

Instead of designing a new punctuation mark for Spanish, it was decided to use an additional question mark, turn it upside down, and place it at the commencement of the phrase.

The same method was applied to the exclamation mark. *¡Qué bien!*

/

SPECIAL USES FOR /

Alternatives: road/rail, June/July

Dates: 23/4/2000

Division: 1/2, 20/20 vision, 50/50 share

Separating lines in poetry:
Why was she born so beautiful/
Why was she born at all

Encasing phonetic symbols: /ðiz/

Apartment number in addresses (Australia): 5/42 Kangaroo Street

Previously used for separating British pounds, shillings and pence: £2/6s/6d

Virgules, slashes,
slants and *strokes,*
Mean/lean
the same to
different folks.

The / is a real **whatchamacallit** of a character.

It was one of the most popular punctuation marks for hundreds of years, and perhaps that is the reason why it has so many names. The original Latin name was *virgula suspensiva*, which means 'raised/poised wand'.

OUR MODERN TERMS FOR IT INCLUDE:

virgule	*oblique*	*slash*
stroke	*diagonal*	*(or forward slash)*
solidus	*slant*	*division sign*

This slanting line has been used variously in the past as a paragraph marker, a full stop, a comma, and a question mark. These days it is mainly used as some

FOR OR AGAINST?

ORIGINAL TEXT:

Trvsty . seldom / to their Friendys vniust
. / Gladd for to helpp . no Crysten cre-
ator / Wyllyng to greve . settyng all yeir
ioy & lust
Only in ye pleasour of god . having no
cvre / Who is most ryche . wth them yey
wylbe sewer / Wher nede is . gevyng
neyther reward ne Fee / Vnreasonably .
Thus lyve prestys . parde . /

sort of divider — between numbers or choices or verse lines or folders in computer hierarchies and internet addresses. It is the slanted line in the % mark, in fractions such as 1/4 and 50/50, and in expressions such as km/h.

The / was used extensively in the Middle Ages to signify a short pause in the text. Some writers went on to use a double // for a longer pause.

In the 1400s the virgule and the full stop were competing with each other, and were often used interchangeably. This made it possible to make 'punctuation riddles' which give a completely different message depending on whether you use the virgules or the full stops.

FOR PRIESTS (FULL STOPS):

Trusty. Seldom to their friends unjust. Glad for to help. No Christian creature willing to grieve. Setting all their joy and desire only in the pleasure of God. Having no care who is most rich. With them they will be sure where need is. Giving neither reward nor fee unreasonably. Thus live priests. In the name of God.

AGAINST PRIESTS (VIRGULES):

Trusty seldom / To their friends unjust / Glad for to help no Christian creature / Willing to grieve setting all their joy and desire - only in the pleasure of God having no care / Who[ever] is most rich with them they will be sure / Where need is, giving neither reward nor fee / Unreasonably thus live priests in the name of God /

S P A C E

B A R

SPECIAL USES FOR

Eight spaces make a TAB on a
conventional typewriter.

Some style manuals recommend
the use of a space to separate
thousands in numbers, for example,
1 000 000 for one million.

Function of the
space:
Nothing takes its
place.

QUICKLY which is the most frequently used key on your keyboard?

CLUE it is also the largest key.

ANSWER the space bar.

Curiously enough, the space between words is also one of the most recent additions to our writing system.

It all began in an Irish monastery just over a thousand years ago.

The alphabet was alive and well, and had been around for a long time. The texts used by the Irish monks were usually written in Latin, in a manner called *scriptura continua*, which meant that the text was written with nospacesatallbetweenthewords.

It is important to know that all writing was intended for oratory use, that is, for reading aloud. Putting spaces between the words had never occurred to anyone: after all, people don't talk with spaces, do they?

There were a handful of punctuation marks that told the monks when to pause and draw a breath and when to raise their voices, but otherwise the text just ran on and on, which was quite suitable for its purpose.

Even so, chanting aloud in a foreign tongue was a pretty tall order for the average Irish monk challenged with LSL (Latin as a Second Language). It was easy to trip over unfamiliar words and botch up the oratory.

One day some of these frustrated monks must have had a brainstorming session. They came up with an idea: 'let's separate the words by inserting a bit of nothing between them'. This could hardly have been seen by the church as responsible financial management, because vellum and parchment were expensive and word spaces, well, took up valuable space — but it worked wonders for Latin chants with an Irish lilt!

The addition of word spaces had another accidental and profoundly revolutionary effect on life and society: it made silent reading possible.

Up until the introduction of word spaces, silent reading was a virtually unknown activity: reading quietly to oneself was simply not done.

On those rare occasions when it did occur, silent reading caused great consternation and amazement. St Augustine describes with almost shocked astonishment how Ambrose, the great Bishop of Milan, could follow the written text with his eyes even as 'his voice and tongue stayed still'.

So next time you press that long thin bar of nothing on your keyboard, remember that
itisallonaccountoftheIrish!

Many computer programs use the ¶ sign to mark the *end* of a paragraph, that is, as a marker for the <ENTER> key.

However, the original use was at the *beginning* of a text, and in the margin.

These two signs form part of the suite of symbols, with the * and †, used instead of numbers to indicate footnotes in the text.

I never use them
I just confuse
them.

155

These two marks clearly have mixed personalities:

The ¶ is called the *paragraph mark* and comes from a *K* meaning 'chapter'.

The § is called the *section mark* and comes from a *G* meaning 'paragraph'.

As explained in the introduction to punctuation, Roman scribes sometimes inserted a *K* for *kaput* ('head') into the text to signify the beginning or 'head' of an argument. The *K* later became a *C* for *capitulum*, signifying 'chapter'. The sign was written with a vertical line through it ₵ to distinguish it from a capital C. The line was doubled and lengthened to ₵, the legs of the 'horseshoe' snipped off neatly, and the round shape filled in, making ¶.

In the second case, *G* stands for the Greek word *graphos*, which means 'writing'. *Paragraphos* means 'beside the text'. A variant of the Greek letter *gamma* was used to mark the beginning of a major section in a manuscript. Both the capital *gamma* Γ, and the lower case *gamma* γ were used, but the capital looked more like Γ in Latin manuscripts.

The curly lower-case paragraph sign started to look like half a 'section' sign §. It is not hard to see where the § comes from.

The
dagger's role
has me
perplexed †

This mark is known as
dagger, obelisk or obelus.

The † and its doubled version
‡ form part of the suite of
symbols, with the *, ¶, and §, used
instead of numbers to indicate
footnotes in the text.

† Until I find the end of text

In old manuscripts this symbol was used to point out something spurious or dubious in a text.

The Greek word *obelós* means a spit for roasting meat. It was at first written ├────┤, perhaps resembling a rotisserie over a fire.

In his *Etymologiae* St Isidore of Seville (*ca* 560–636) describes the sharp, spear-like qualities of the obelus in his notes about critical marks:

> The Obelus [...] is placed against words or sententiae repeated unnecessarily or in those places where a recording is noted for its falsity so that a kind of arrow may slit the throat of what is superfluous and penetrate to the vitals of what is false.

After some time, the spit acquired two dots and was made to stand up on its end instead ├∸┤ ∴

When the character lost its end-pieces and the dots moved up-wards, ∴ the step wasn't far to the † symbol we know today.

The sign is still called obelus or obelisk by some people, but is better known as the dagger. Nowadays the dagger is most commonly used as a reference mark, much like the asterisk. Its old role as an indicator of a corrupt or doubtful statement can still be seen in language books, for example, 'Sentences such as

†*I drunk it*

are common in some dialects, but are considered non-standard'.

In mathematics, the division sign when written ÷ is also derived from the early form of obelus. This character is much younger than the obelus, however, dating back to the mid-17th century.

Nice and round
and strong and
stark
Is the European
... Mark?

NEW KEY ON THE BLOCK

A recent character on the computer keyboard (or through key combinations, character codes or downloaded fonts) is the new symbol for a major currency: the euro.

In the European Commission's own words, the euro symbol:

> … *was inspired by the Greek letter epsilon, in reference to the cradle of European civilisation and to the first letter of the word 'Europe'. The parallel lines represent the stability of the euro. The euro sign is easily recognisable and in a few years' time will be as well known as the dollar sign ($). As an abbreviation, the sign is very convenient and it will very soon be on every new computer or typewriter keyboard.*

The euro sign is an officially registered mark, unlike such universally known currency symbols as the dollar and yen signs, which have never been registered.

No effort was spared when it came to the design of euro notes and coins. Take the euro series of coins: the design of the new common European small change started in the northern spring of 1996, when the European Commission was given a mandate to stage a design competition that would eventually culminate in a winning design of the new European currency. In the next few months, thirty-six designs were received.

On 13 March 1997 a jury of artists, designers, numismatists and consumers picked out a shortlist of the nine best entries. To ensure complete anonymity, all traces of the originators and even the nationality of the submitted designs had been carefully removed by a *huissier de justice*.

After this, 2000 people from various backgrounds were surveyed for their reactions to the designs. There were two clear favourites.

Blind and vision-impaired people were also consulted.

Based on the comments of all these people, the winning series was selected.

The designer, Mr Luc Luycx, a thirty-nine-year-old Belgian computer scientist, got a bit more than the small change he had drawn: he was given € 24,000 for his trouble.

The final design of the European banknotes was selected in a similar way. Mr Robert Kalina of the Austrian Central Bank was announced as the winner in December 1996.

Character codes

and

  combinations

combinations

This section shows how to access many of the non-keyboard characters covered in this book (and some that are not covered). For information on how to access characters not included in this list, consult your instruction manuals or the many resources available on the internet.

NOTES
- HTML CODE
  HTML code can be written using either the HTML and ISO Latin 1 code. For example, Smörgåsbord can be written either Smörgåsbord (HTML) or Smörgåsbord (ISO Latin 1).

- NUMBER CODES ON THE PC
  On the PC, hold down the <Alt> key, then enter the number code on the numeric keypad. When you release the <Alt> key, the character will appear on the screen.

- KEY COMBINATIONS ON THE MACINTOSH
  On the Macintosh there are three possible key combinations —

\<option\> plus another key

> *For instance, to write a pound sign, hold down the \<option\> key, then press 3*

\<option\> and \<shift\> plus another key

For instance, to write an inverted question mark, hold down the \<option\> and \<shift\> keys, then press the ? key

\<option\> and \<another key\> followed by \<a third key\>

For instance, to write a Ü, hold down the \<option\> key and press the \<u\> key. Release both. Nothing will happen. Now type an upper-case \<U\>. The U will appear on the screen and will have an umlaut above it.

In the following tables some of the codes or key combinations may differ, or be unavailable, with variations in platforms, operating systems, software or browsers.

n/a	indicates when a particular character/symbol is known to be unavailable.
*	indicates a character that is defined in HTML 3.2. Older browsers will not read this character properly.
* *	indicates a character that is not part of ISO Latin 1, and might not work on all platforms.

PUNCTUATION MARKS

Character and name		HTML	ISO Latin 1	PC	Macintosh
¶	paragraph	¶*	&#182;	Alt+0182	Option 7
§	section	§*	&#167;	Alt+0167	Option 6
¡	inverted exclamation mark	¡*	&#161;	Alt+0161	Option 1
¿	inverted question mark	¿*	&#191;	Alt+0191	Option shift ?
«	left guillemet	«*	&#171;	Alt+0171	Option \
»	right guillemet	»*	&#187;	Alt+0187	Option shift |
...	ellipsis	n/a	&#133;	Alt+0133	Option ;
·	middle dot	·*	&#183;	Alt+0183	Option shift (
—	em rule or dash	—**	n/a	Alt+0151	Option shift _
–	en rule or dash	–**	n/a	Alt+0150	Option -

SYMBOLS

Character and name		HTML	ISO Latin 1	PC	Macintosh
†	dagger	†**	n/a	Alt+0134	Option t
‡	double dagger	‡**	n/a	Alt+0135	Option shift &
£	pound	£*	&#163;	Alt+0163	Option 3
¥	yen	¥*	&#165;	Alt+0165	Option y
¤	general currency sign (may also create other currency signs, depending on platform)	¤*	&#164;	Alt+0164	Option shift @
¢	cent	¢*	&#162;	Alt+0162	Option 4
÷	division mark	÷*	&#247;	Alt+0247	Option /
×	multiplication mark	×*	&#215;	Alt+0215	n/a
©	copyright	©*	&#169;	Alt+0169	Option g
®	registered trade mark	®*	&#174;	Alt+0174	Option r
°	degree	°*	&#176;	Alt+0176	Option shift *
±	plus or minus	±*	&#177;	Alt+0177	Option shift +
¬	not	¬*	&#172;	Alt+0172	Option l
µ	micro	µ*	&#181;	Alt+0181	Option m

NUMERALS

Character and name		HTML	ISO Latin 1	PC	Macintosh
$1/4$	fraction one-fourth	¼*	&#188;	Alt+0188	n/a
$1/2$	fraction one-half	½*	&#189;	Alt+0189	n/a
$3/4$	fraction three-fourths	¾*	&#190;	Alt+0190	n/a
^{1}	superscript one	¹*	&#185;	Alt+0185	n/a
^{2}	superscript two	²*	&#178;	Alt+0178	n/a
^{3}	superscript three	³*	&#179;	Alt+0179	n/a

ORDINALS

Character and name		HTML	ISO Latin 1	PC	Macintosh
^{a}	feminine	ª*	&#170;	Alt+0170	Option 9
^{o}	masculine	º*	&#186;	Alt+0186	Option 0

DIACRITICS WITH LETTERS

Character and name		HTML	ISO Latin 1	PC	Macintosh
Á	acute accent	&Aacute;	&#193;	Alt+0193	
á		&aacute;	&#225;	Alt+0225	
É		&Eacute;	&#201;	Alt+0201	
é		&eacute;	&#233;	Alt+0233	Option
Í		&Iacute;	&#205;	Alt+0205	e
í		&iacute;	&#237;	Alt+0237	then
Ó		&Oacute;	&#211;	Alt+0211	letter
ó		&oacute;	&#243;	Alt+0243	
Ú		&Uacute;	&#218;	Alt+0218	
ú		&uacute;	&#250;	Alt+0250	
Å	angstrom (ring above)	&Aring;	&#197;	Alt+0197	Option shift A
å		&aring;	&#229;	Alt+0229	Option a
Ç	cedilla	&Ccedil;	&#199;	Alt+0199	Option shift C
ç		&ccedil;	&#231;	Alt+0231	Option c

Character and name		HTML	ISO Latin 1	PC	Macintosh
Â	circumflex	&Acirc;	&#194;	Alt+0194	
â		&acirc;	&#226;	Alt+0226	
Ê		&Ecirc;	&#202;	Alt+0202	
ê		&ecirc;	&#234;	Alt +0234	Option
Î		&Icirc;	&#206;	Alt+0206	i
î		&icirc;	&#238;	Alt+0238	then
Ô		&Ocirc;	&#212;	Alt+0212	letter
ô		&ocirc;	&#244;	Alt+0244	
Û		&Ucirc;	&#219;	Alt+0219	
û		&ucirc;	&#251;	Alt+0251	
À	grave accent	&Agrave;	&#192;	Alt+0192	
à		&agrave;	&#224;	Alt+0224	
È		&Egrave;	&#200;	Alt+0200	
è		&egrave;	&#232;	Alt+0232	Option
Ì		&Igrave;	&#204;	Alt+0204	`
ì		&igrave;	&#236;	Alt+0236	then
Ò		&Ograve;	&#210;	Alt+0210	letter
ò		&ograve;	&#242;	Alt+0242	
Ù		&Ugrave;	&#217;	Alt+0217	
ù		&ugrave;	&#249;	Alt+0249	
Ã	tilde	&Atilde;	&#195;	Alt+0195	
ã		&atilde;	&#227;	Alt+0227	Option
Ñ		&Ntilde;	&#209;	Alt+0209	n
ñ		&ntilde;	&#241;	Alt+0241	then
Õ		&Otilde;	&#213;	Alt+0213	letter
õ		&otilde;	&#245;	Alt+0245	
Ä	umlaut (diaeresis)	&Auml;	&#196;	Alt+0196	
ä		&auml;	&#228;	Alt+0228	
Ë		&Euml;	&#203;	Alt+0203	
ë		&euml;	&#235;	Alt+0235	Option
Ï		&Iuml;	&#207;	Alt+0207	u
ï		&iuml;	&#239;	Alt+0239	then
Ö		&Ouml;	&#214;	Alt+0214	letter
ö		&ouml;	&#246;	Alt+0246	
Ü		&Uuml;	&#220;	Alt+0220	
ü		&uuml;	&#252;	Alt+0252	
ÿ		&yuml;	&#255;	Alt+0255	

DIACRITICS WITHOUT LETTERS

Character and name		HTML	ISO Latin 1	PC	Macintosh
´	acute accent	&acute;	&#180;	Alt+0180	Option shift E
¸	cedilla	&cedil;	&#184;	Alt+0184	n/a
¯	macron	&macr;	&#175;	Alt+0175	Option shift <
¨	umlaut (diaeresis)	&uml;	&#168;	Alt+0168	Option shift U

LIGATURES

Character and name		HTML	ISO Latin 1	PC	Macintosh
Æ	A+E	&AElig;	&#198;	Alt+0198	Option shift '
æ		&aelig;	&#230;	Alt+0230	Option '
fi	f+i	n/a	n/a	n/a	Option shift %
fl	f+l	n/a	n/a	n/a	Option shift ^
Œ	O+E	n/a	n/a	Alt+0140	Option shift Q
œ		n/a	n/a	Alt+0156	Option q
ß	s+s	&szlig;	&#223;	Alt+0223	Option s

OTHER

Character and name		HTML	ISO Latin 1	PC	Macintosh
Ð	eth	&ETH;	&#208;	Alt+0208	n/a
ð		&eth;	&#240;	Alt+0240	n/a
Ø	o with oblique stroke	&Oslash;	&#216;	Alt+0216	Option shift O
ø		&oslash;	&#248;	Alt+0248	Option o
þ	thorn	&THORN;	&#222;	Alt+0222	n/a
þ		&thorn;	&#254;	Alt+0254	n/a

ALLEN TO WORTHAM

Sources

NOTE

The sources below have been given using the author-date (Harvard) system of citations. Internet sources have been given according to the system recommended by the Network Working Group in the standards document RFC1738 along with the MLA and APA recommendations of adding access dates.

Allen, J., 1997, *Symbols, Accents, and Funky Characters*, URL: <http://hotwired.lycos.com/webmonkey/97/36/index3a.html?tw=aut horing>, 11 Sep. (accessed 05 Jan. 2001).

Baird, K., 1998, *Special Characters in HTML*, URL: <http://www.utexas.edu/learn/pub/spchar/>, 02 Mar. (accessed 05 Jan. 2001).

Barber, C. L., 1967 [1964], *The Story of Language*, 4th printing, Pan Books Ltd, London.

Barnhart, R. K. (ed.), 1988, *The Barnhart Dictionary of Etymology*, H. W. Wilson Co., New York.

Beeching, W. A., 1974, *Century of the Typewriter*, William Heinemann Ltd, London.

Bemer, R. W., 2000, *How ASCII Got its Backslash*, URL: <http://www.bobbemer.com/BACSLASH.HTM>, 10 Jun. (accessed 05 Jan. 2001).

Berners-Lee, T., Masinter, L., McCahill, M., 1994, 'APPENDIX: Recommendations for URLs in Context', in *Uniform Resource Locators (URL)*, Document RFC1738, Network Working Group, URL: <ftp://ftp.demon.co.uk/pub/doc/rfc/rfc1738.txt>, Dec. (accessed 07 Oct. 2000).

Bonfante, L., 1990, *Etruscan*, Reading the Past series, British Museum Publications Ltd, London.

Brader, M., 1998, *Origin of the Dollar Sign*, URL:

<http://homepages.tcp.co.uk/~laker/faq/faq.html>, Dec. (accessed 05 Jan. 2001).

Budge, Sir E. A. W., 1989 [1910], *Egyptian Language*, 3rd edn, Routledge, London.

—— , 1967 [1895], *The Egyptian Book of the Dead* (*The Papyrus of Ani*), reprint, Dover Publications, Inc., New York.

Chauvier, J. H., 1848, *A Treatise on Punctuation* (transl. J. H. Huntington, from French), Simpkin, Marshall & Co., London.

Clanchy, M. T., 1979, *From Memory to Written Record*, Edward Arnold (Publishers) Ltd, London.

Cook, B. F., 1987, *Greek Inscriptions*, Reading the Past series, British Museum Publications Ltd, London.

Crystal, D., 1995, *The Cambridge Encyclopedia of the English Language*, Cambridge University Press.

—— , 1997, *The Cambridge Encyclopedia of Language*, 2nd edn, Cambridge University Press.

Crystal, D. and Crystal, H., 2000, *Words on Words: Quotations about Language and Languages*, Penguin.

Davies, W. V., 1990, 'Egyptian Hieroglyphs', in *Reading the Past*, British Museum Publications.

Émigré Fonts Special Features: Mrs Eaves, 1995, URL: <http://www.emigre.com/FeME.html>, Émigré Graphics (accessed 05 Jan. 2001).

Encyclopedia of Ideas, 1991 [1983 as *The Macquarie History of Ideas*], Macquarie Library.

European Commission 2000, *Questions & Answers on the euro and European Economic and Monetary Union*, URL: <http://europa.eu.int/euro/quest/>, 10 May (accessed 05 Jan. 2001).

Fitzpatrick, John C., 1907, 'Spanish Galleons and Pieces of Eight', in *Scribner's Magazine*, November.

Glaister, G. A., 1996, *Encyclopedia of the Book*, 2nd edn, Oak Knoll Press, New Castle, Delaware, USA & The British Library, London.

Graden, P., 1983, 'Punctuation in a Middle English Sermon', in *Five Hundred Years of Words and Sounds*, D. S. Brewer, Cambridge.

Haley, A., 1995, *Alphabet: the History, Evolution and Design of the Letters We Use Today*, Thames & Hudson, London.

Healey, J. F., 1990, 'The Early Alphabet', in *Reading the Past*, British Museum Publications.

Herron, S., 2000, *A Natural History of the @ Sign*, URL: <http://www.herodios.com/herron_tc/atsign.html> (accessed 05 Jan. 2001).

Hirsch, R., 1978, *The Printed Word: its Impact and Diffusion*, Variorum Reprints, London.

Irwin, K. G., 1958, *Man Learns to Write*, Dobson Books, London.

Jean, G., 1992, *Writing: the Story of Alphabets and Scripts* (transl. Jenny Oates), New Horizons series, Thames & Hudson, London.

Jensen, H., 1970, *Sign, Symbol and Script: an Account of Man's Efforts to Write* (transl. from German by George Unwin), George Allen & Unwin Ltd., London.

Kahn, J. E. (ed.), 1985, *The Right Word at the Right Time*, The Reader's Digest Association Limited, London.

Korpela, J., 2000, *The ISO Latin 1 Character Repertoire — a Description with Usage Notes*, URL: <http://www.hut.fi/u/jkorpela/latin1/>, 28 Sep. (accessed 05 Jan. 2001).

Lancon, D., Jr., 1999, *HTML Character Codes*, URL: <http://www.obkb.com/dcljr/charstxt.html > (accessed 05 Jan. 2001).

Levarie, N., 1982, *The Art & History of Books*, reprint, Da Capo, New York.

McCrum, R., Cran, W. & MacNeil, R., 1992, *The Story of English*, 2nd edn, Faber & Faber, London.

Naveh, J., 1975, *Origins of the Alphabet*, Cassell's Introducing Archaeology Series – Book Six, Cassell & Company, London.

Ouaknin, M.-A., 1999, *Mysteries of the Alphabet: the origins of writing*, Abbeville Press Publishers.

Parkes, M. B., 1992, *Pause and Effect: an Introduction to the History of Punctuation in the West*, Scolar Press, Aldershot, Hants., UK.

Partridge, E., 1961, *Comic Alphabets*, Routledge & Kegan Paul, London, Copyright © 1961 (reprinted by permission of Sheil Land Associates, London).

Peters, P., 1995, *The Cambridge Australian English Style Guide*, Cambridge University Press.

Polt, R., *A Brief History of Typewriters*, URL: <http://xavier.xu.edu/~polt/tw-history.html>, undated (accessed 05 Jan. 2001).

Quinion, M. B., 1999, *Signs for Sums: Where our Arithmetic Symbols Come from*, URL:<http://www.worldwidewords.org/articles/signs.htm>, 05 Jun. (accessed 05 Jan. 2001).

—— , 1996, *Where it's at: Names for a Common Symbol*, URL: <http://www.worldwidewords.org/articles/whereat,htm>, 24 Aug. (accessed 05 Jan. 2001).

Rehr, D., *The First Typewriter*, URL: <http://home.earthlink.net/~dcrehr/firsttw.html>, undated (accessed 05 Jan. 2001).

—— , *Consider QWERTY*, URL: <http://home.earthlink.net/~dcrehr/whyqwert.html>, undated (accessed 05 Jan. 2001).

Richards, G. T., 1964 [1938], *The History and Development of Typewriters*, 2nd edn, Science Museum, London.

Robertson, P., 1974, *The Shell Book of Firsts*, Ebury Press & Michael Joseph Ltd, London.

Robinson, A., 1995, *The Story of Writing*, Thames & Hudson Ltd, London.

Romano, F. J. & Romano, R. M., 1998, *The GATF Encyclopedia of Graphic Communications*, GATF Press, Pittsburgh, USA.

Scott, B. M., 1999, Re: *Concerning the name of the letter "W" etc.*, URL: <http://x38.deja.com/=dnc/[ST_rn=ps]/getdoc.xp?AN=527223782>, 19 Sep. Deja.com, Inc. (accessed 05 Jan. 2001).

United States Patents and Trademarks Office, 2000, *Databases: Patents* Full-Text and Bibliographic, URL:

<http://www.uspto.gov/patft/index.html> (accessed 05 Jan. 2001).

Webmonkey, 2000, *Reference: Special Characters*, URL:
   <http://hotwired.lycos.com/webmonkey/reference/special_
   characters/>, Wired Digital Inc. (accessed 05 Jan. 2001).

Williams, R., 1995, *The Little Mac Book*, 4th edn, Peachpit Press, Berkeley,
   California.

Wortham, J., *A Pickle for the Knowing Ones*, URL:
   <http://www.usd.edu/~jwortham/jackdaw/pickle.html>, undated
   (accessed 05 Jan. 2001).

FOR THE BEST IN PAPERBACKS, LOOK FOR THE

In every corner of the world, on every subject under the sun, Penguin represents quality and variety—the very best in publishing today.

For complete information about books available from Penguin—including Penguin Classics, Penguin Compass, and Puffins—and how to order them, write to us at the appropriate address below. Please note that for copyright reasons the selection of books varies from country to country.

In the United States: Please write to *Penguin Group (USA), P.O. Box 12289 Dept. B, Newark, New Jersey 07101-5289* or call 1-800-788-6262.

In the United Kingdom: Please write to *Dept. EP, Penguin Books Ltd, Bath Road, Harmondsworth, West Drayton, Middlesex UB7 0DA.*

In Canada: Please write to *Penguin Books Canada Ltd, 10 Alcorn Avenue, Suite 300, Toronto, Ontario M4V 3B2.*

In Australia: Please write to *Penguin Books Australia Ltd, P.O. Box 257, Ringwood, Victoria 3134.*

In New Zealand: Please write to *Penguin Books (NZ) Ltd, Private Bag 102902, North Shore Mail Centre, Auckland 10.*

In India: Please write to *Penguin Books India Pvt Ltd, 11 Panchsheel Shopping Centre, Panchsheel Park, New Delhi 110 017.*

In the Netherlands: Please write to *Penguin Books Netherlands bv, Postbus 3507, NL-1001 AH Amsterdam.*

In Germany: Please write to *Penguin Books Deutschland GmbH, Metzlerstrasse 26, 60594 Frankfurt am Main.*

In Spain: Please write to *Penguin Books S. A., Bravo Murillo 19, 1° B, 28015 Madrid.*

In Italy: Please write to *Penguin Italia s.r.l., Via Benedetto Croce 2, 20094 Corsico, Milano.*

In France: Please write to *Penguin France, Le Carré Wilson, 62 rue Benjamin Baillaud, 31500 Toulouse.*

In Japan: Please write to *Penguin Books Japan Ltd, Kaneko Building, 2-3-25 Koraku, Bunkyo-Ku, Tokyo 112.*

In South Africa: Please write to *Penguin Books South Africa (Pty) Ltd, Private Bag X14, Parkview, 2122 Johannesburg.*